Industrial Revolution

The Fine Line Between Digital Innovations

(Embracing Disruption and Thriving in the Age of Technology)

James Tanner

Published By **Elena Holly**

James Tanner

All Rights Reserved

Industrial Revolution: The Fine Line Between Digital Innovations (Embracing Disruption and Thriving in the Age of Technology)

ISBN 978-0-9950956-5-6

No part of this guidebook shall be reproduced in any form without permission in writing from the publisher except in the case of brief quotations embodied in critical articles or reviews.

Legal & Disclaimer

The information contained in this book is not designed to replace or take the place of any form of medicine or professional medical advice. The information in this book has been provided for educational & entertainment purposes only.

The information contained in this book has been compiled from sources deemed reliable, and it is accurate to the best of the Author's knowledge; however, the Author cannot guarantee its accuracy and validity and cannot be held liable for any errors or omissions. Changes are periodically made to this book. You must consult your doctor or get professional medical advice before using any of the suggested remedies, techniques, or information in this book.

Upon using the information contained in this book, you agree to hold harmless the Author from and against any damages, costs, and expenses, including any legal fees potentially resulting from the application of any of the information provided by this guide. This disclaimer applies to any damages or injury caused by the use and application, whether directly or indirectly, of any advice or information presented, whether for breach of contract, tort, negligence, personal injury, criminal intent, or under any other cause of action.

You agree to accept all risks of using the information presented inside this book. You need to consult a professional medical practitioner in order to ensure you are both able and healthy enough to participate in this program.

Table Of Contents

Chapter 1: Prelude To Industrialization 1

Chapter 2: The Arrival Of Steam Power .. 10

Chapter 3: The Industrial Revolution Takes Control 19

Chapter 4: The 2nd Industrial Revolution 33

Chapter 5: The Consumer Society 41

Chapter 6: The Industrial Society 52

Chapter 7: War And Peace In The Future 62

Chapter 8: The Timeline And The Changes That Occurred In The Industrial Revolution 73

Chapter 9: Broken Down Per Market 81

Chapter 10: Social And Societal Results Of The Revolution 107

Chapter 11: Transport 137

Chapter 1: Prelude To Industrialization

"With the newly discovered Romancrank] and connecting rod system all the elements needed for building the steam engine (invented around 1712) The aeolipile of Hero (generating steam-powered power) along with the cylinder as well as piston (in metallic force pumps) and the valves that do not return (in water pumps) and gearing (in water mills as well as clocks) The rod system was recognized from Roman the time of "Roman times."

Tullia Ritti, Klaus Grewe and Paul Kessener, The Roman World 44 BC-AD 180.

The development of technology has been advancing over many thousands of years. In particular, using an advanced combination of pulleys and ropes as well as gears, levers and locking mechanisms Romans employed these devices for construction, at the

Colosseum to change the scenery as well as for their war machine.

An essential steam engine was invented around 2,000 years ago, in the 1st century CE. The engine was named Hero's due to the fact that it was developed in the name of Hero from Alexandria and was referred to as an aeolipile early machine, it was an engine that used steam. The ball was circular that was held to its place by two pipes that were placed on either side. The ball was filled up with pressured steam that was pumped by the pipe. The steam exited the ball through two different exhaust pipes. Once steam was released in this way the ball swung between the pipes, and then rotated.

There was never any real application for the device, following the fall of the Roman Empire there was no interest considered its effects.

"[Hero's steam engine"Hero's steam engine"

a technological invention to find a divine truth hidden in the laws of heavens.

Thus by observing this small and quite short test, can we understand and evaluate the powerful and amazing nature of the heavens, as well as the nature of winds."

Vitruvius

However, there was a second important element in the Industrial Revolution that was being gradually developed, and that included a better understanding of gears, as well as the conversion of vertical motion to horizontal movement. Additionally, engineers were studying how to manage the forces.

Water power, and the water wheel particularly, played an significant roles right until the beginning in the Industrial Revolution and they would continue to be utilized even after the development of steam energy.

The first waterwheel was an horizontal one that was directly linked with the millstone. The date is approximately 250 BCE. The wheel was located beneath the mill, and was it was turned by a stream of water. It was situated above the gristmill inside the millhouse. The water wheel was a basic model with numerous limitations because it was not equipped with gears and the rotation of the millstone depended upon the current of water.

About 200 years later, vertical water wheels came into usage by the Romans as well as other people. They could be used for a wide range of designs, as well as shifting and a lot more control. In the 3rd century CE in the 3rd Century CE, the Romans were building the first sawmill, driven by a waterwheel.

The gristmills that were powered by water became widespread from that time up to the point to the point that there were more than 5 000 mills operating in England at the time of 1100 CE which is one mill per 300 persons. Just two hundred years later, there were nearly 17,000 mills operating in England which were being utilized for various purposes.

Then there was another vital element which was beginning to take form. The clock. The precise operation of the clock as well as the timing of its operation would be essential in the development of technology as well as the world of mechanical technology. It was ironic that the very different view of the world which resulted from the findings from Isaac Newton and the acceptance of the concept of a heliocentric (or sun-centered) solar system was founded partially on the exact geometries of Ptolemy who's geocentric universe had been rejected.

Ptolemy's geometry of heaven that described an earth-centered universe, was built upon a variety of perfectly formed circles. The scientists of that time were of the belief that Heavens were part of a space beyond Earth and believed that the moon, sun, the planets and stars were in perfect order and impermanent. They all performed perfectly in flawless circles. In order for Ptolemy's calculation to be effective the way he wanted, he needed to take several circles away from the center and create circles within epicycles, also known as circles. The descriptions of Ptolemy's celestial entities was extremely accurate. it was not until somewhat more exact estimation of the length one year was demanded and his method was replaced by Copernicus.

However, while his account of Heaven's was later removed, the geometrical and the movements he talked about worked very well in the articulation of machines particularly clocks. In the year around 1300 CE in Europe The first massive Astronomical clocks were being made. They were precise mechanical instruments built on the Ptolemy's geocentric solar device, i.e., his epicycles as well as his off-center gears. It was the popularity of these clocks as well as their capacity to anticipate the motions of planets that led the believers to accept a physical universe in which God was the "Great Watchmaker'. This notion of a world made by mechanical technology was the catalyst for the development of advanced industrial machinery with intricate mechanical gearing, timing or clock-like mechanisms were essential.

"Most of the earliest clocks weren't so just chronometers, but rather displays of the patterns of the universe It is evident that the genesis of mechanical clocks are within a vast universe of gigantic planetaria an equatoria-based astrolabe, as well as geared ones." (ED: The clocks were constructed by using the geocentric Ptolemaic method.It was

Lynn White Jr.

DID THE INDUSTRIAL REVOLUTION START WITH THE STEAM ENGINE?

While for many historians that the Industrial Revolution starts with the steam engine, the actual process was in the beginning.

The textile industry of the 17th century were developed that operated using the power of water wheels. The water wheel was comprehended at the time and there was various designs that took advantage of the water flow within a specific river. Additionally, factory owners had an advanced grasp of the process used to convert the power of rotation from the wheel of water into precisely repeated movements required by their weaving machines. This isn't an accident that the production of textiles in a sense, sparked an Industrial Revolution, meaning that manufacturing textiles was one of the first processes that was converted into mechanical movements and the machinery that subsequently resulted.

The process was carried out using a grid made up consisting of lengthwise fixed threads referred to by the name of warp. The weft (also called "the woof") was then placed at 90 degrees to the warp, and then pulled the warp, then put under the warp. This made it the ideal grid for use with machinery.

It's also no coincidence that the most significant part of the history of computers began by using textile machines. Joseph Marie Jacquard invented the Jacquard weaving loom in 1804. It was a loom which was controlled by a series of cards with instructions to weave intricate designs. The "father of computers" Charles Babbage owned one of Jacquard's complicated fabrics which was created by punch cards. He took it to use as inspiration as trying to design the first computer that could be programmed during the 1830s. However, the project was never completed. As a finalized design, Babbage intended to utilize his punch cards system from Jacquard to manage his mechanical computer.

Chapter 2: The Arrival Of Steam Power

"I was out for an excursion on a beautiful Sabbath day. I was in the Green of Glasgow at the gate located at the end of Charlotte Street -- had been through the old wash-house. I was thinking about engines at that time when I arrived to the house of the herd, at which point it occurred to my head that since steam is an elastic substance it would flow into a vacuum. And should a connection be established between the cylinder and an exhausted vessel, it would enter the vessel, and could be condensed without cooling the engine. Then I realized that I had to rid myself of the steam that had condensed and the injection water, if I employed the jet method, which is used in Newcomen's engines. Two methods of achieving it occurred to me. One is, water can be discharged via a descending pipe in the event that an outlet can be found at depths of 35 to 36 feet. Then, any air can be extracted with an insignificant pump. Another option was to build the pump sufficiently large that it could extract water as well as air. I'd never walked any beyond the golf-house, when everything was planned within my head."

James Watt

In Robert Hart's words an remembrance of the details of Watt's inspiration moment that occurred in the month of May 1765 in order to enhance Thomas Newcomen's steam-powered engine.[In Robert Hart's words, a recollection of Watt's moment of

In 1687, Isaac Newton published, Philosophiae Naturalis Principia Mathematica (Mathematical Principles of Natural Philosophy). The book was later referred to in the form of Principia. Many experts consider it as the greatest scientific work, Newton described the forces that controlled the universe and the oceans, as well as the tides and the various objects on Earth and the planets, using mathematical precision.

The precision and scope of his research led him to the conviction that the universe was known and machinable. The belief in this was as crucial as the findings he made. The work of his team suggested that human beings might, through careful observation and a rigorous scientific approach, develop effective devices, and possibly also, conquer nature's deadly forces.

Twenty-five years after Newton's publication of his Principia, Thomas Newcomen invented the very first working steam engine. The device was simple and consisted of two chambers as well as four valves. In one chamber, the firebox was heated by water in a different chamber. It was then able to release pressurized steam in a chamber that had the form of a piston once the valve was opened. The steam moved the piston towards the highest point of the chamber. Then the valve shut, and another valve opened that let cool water flow into the chamber of the piston condensing the steam, as well as creating a vacuum such that the piston fell to the floor of the chamber. The first time the engine was created it was attached to an oscillating beam connected to a pump which could draw water out of coal mines.

The steam engine in question was not efficient. It was not a big make a difference. The primary use for it was coal mines with tons of coal to fuel the firebox. It was, however, not suitable for other uses.

In 1781, James Watt offered his improved model. The steam engine was two times as effective, meaning steam was now to maturity and was able to be utilized for many different purposes.

It was believed that the Watt steam engine had an condenser. Instead of spraying cold water into the piston chamber steam that was hot was drawn through the condenser. The piston chamber was not able to get as hot as it did prior to and significantly increased the performance. Watt's change was simple which is why a large portion of the Newcomen's engines were fitted with the condenser of Watt.

Watt kept improving his engine over the following 40 years. The improvements he made to steam engines suitable to be used for many tasks. The designs he later developed resulted in rotary motion instead of employing the oscillating beam from Newcomen's engine. It meant that the research and expertise of engineering that was developed by the wheel of water could be incorporated into steam engines. In the future, massive engines will be able to power a range of manufacturing facilities.

Watt's steam engines were legendary. His Grazebrook Engine, for example was among the biggest ever constructed and operated for nearly 100 years within Birmingham in which it was utilized for provide oxygen to blast furnaces, which significantly improved the quality of iron produced.

Even though Newcomen and Watt began the development of steam engines There were many kinds of steam engines, which were more advanced and complex when they advanced. The initial engine developed that was developed by Newcomen was referred to as The Newcomen Atmospheric Engine. It was atmospheric since it relied on the variation in pressure of the atmosphere to propel the piston to the lowest point of the cylinder, after the water was cold and had formed the vacuum. Watt's engine was based on the same principles, but they had a higher efficiency. The atmospheric engines were not particularly efficient, and therefore high-pressure steam engines that reciprocated were invented.

Watt has deliberately stayed clear of creating these due to concerns about safety. Also, in the very beginning days of high pressure engines, a number of them have exploded, killing quite many individuals. The high pressure was able to allow the development of stationary horizontal engines that were tiny, strong effective and efficient, as well as providing steady speed. Compound engines followed, which used the steam that was originally hot multiple times in order to boost effectiveness and power. They were employed in the shipping industry and numerous ships of World War Two used these engines like those of the Victory Ships and Liberty Ships manufactured by the United States.

From 1950 onwards, steam was widely used throughout the world. As an example, steam shovels and steam cranes were vital in the field of construction, like during the construction of the Panama Canal. Steam locomotives today are utilized across Cuba, Serbia, Indonesia, India, and China. Steam technology is extensively used for the generation of electricity. The majority of power plants located in the United States, including nuclear power stations, utilize steam turbines for power generation.

Nuclear submarines and ships utilize steam turbines for powering their ships. In addition, there are some older vessels that are operated by steam engine.

Steam power was an exciting prospect for the technology, a major shift was taking place that would become an integral aspect in the Industrial Revolution.

Due to a myriad of factors that led to the development of textiles, it became the very first industry that shift to a factory-based. Numerous inventions had taken place in the second half during the late 18th century, which made it easier to make textiles. The inventions of the Spinning Jenny, and later the more modern Water Frame made strong durable threads in just a smaller amount of time it would have taken prior to. Also, it became apparent that looms could turn into factories. The grid-like pattern of weaving and the regular movements involved in weaving seemed to be perfect to create the first significant industrial sector that was factory-based. In 1835, there were more than 11,000 power looms operating in Britain. They were exported to across the globe as well as the raw materials of Britain's vast global empire were sent to England to be woven.

Thanks to Englishmen Isaac Newton, Newcomen and Watt together with the well advanced textile manufacturing industry and the highly developed textile industry, the Industrial Revolution began in England and over the following seventy years it was almost exclusively to England. It was unable to expand across the globe initially as the British government stifled the export of equipment and data about its technologies. England recognized that the state-of-the art manufacturing technology provided it with a major advantage over its competitors and was one of main reasons why England could capitalize on and grow its empire and influence in the Victorian period.

Chapter 3: The Industrial Revolution Takes Control

"Already the steam engine works in our mines, propels vessels, dredges our ports as well as our rivers fabricates iron, creates timber, mills grain spins and weaves our clothes, carries the greatest burdens. It is believed that the steam engine will one day become an all-purpose motor or be used to replace animals, waterfalls and air flows."

Sadi Carnot, circa 1824

It wasn't evident the power of steam would change the entire world. It was mostly used to remove flooded coal mines. The steam engines were big in weight, but they were also constrained in their ability to perform.

As they developed, a whole technology was developed around their technology. Steam engines will be less bulky and more technologically advanced. They could also be designed to be able to do a wide range of movements. At some point the inventor realized they could be placed in a mobile platform.

A. English inventor Richard Trevithick built a number of tiny steam engines with high pressure during the latter part of the 1700s. They could be transported to the customer via the form of a cart pulled by horses. In 1801 Trevithick created what he described as the steam-powered carriage, also called a "puffer" and was able to drive it through in the city in Camborne, England on Christmas Eve. It was possibly the first automobile that was self-powered. In 1804 Trevithick created and ran the first working train in England. Trevithick fitted a huge high-pressure engine in his locomotive which proved that steam power could be adaptable and can be used with a variety of methods.

The first working steam engine was designed by George Stephenson and his son Robert in 1814. The engine was designed for hauling coal. In 1829, the well-known

Rocket locomotive was designed by the same group. It had a boiler with multiple tubes and was made standard following the fact.

The future of locomotives wasn't yet a sealed deal. The same year, 1829 The infamous Rainhill Trials occurred near Liverpool in England. Five locomotives vied to be awarded a contract. However, they were required to show that they were better to move freight over an engine with a stationary steam that moved cars across the track with the pulley system. The Rocket proved to be a success and was the only one that did not fail. The event was attended by more than 10,000 participants. event and the race was watched by many of the world's most famous engineers and steam engines enthusiasts of the day.

At the time, there was only 50 miles of tracks within England. Two decades later England was home to more than 6,600 miles of track. And at the time of 1890, there were around three thousand miles of track. As England has a distance of 600 miles in length and 227 wide in its broadest it meant that the rail could be able to reach almost any place in the Island.

Before the engine, a steamboat was first invented. Shortly after the invention of the Newcomen steam engine, engineers attempted to mount it on the small vessel. The engine was constructed for stationary use and created many problems when it was mounted on the case of a boat that was moving. It was large, heavy and it caused the boat to move. But, many patents were granted for an engine powered Newcomen boat in 1729-1736. But, the Newcomen engine worked efficiently on large vessels and a number of patents were issued in 1783, including one made by an Frenchman from 1783. Then, a few years later, an American invented his own model and operated a passenger line during a period of time - proving the practicality of it.

It was the other American Robert Fulton, to develop a functioning steamboat with an Watt steam engine. The new steamboat he built was named North River Steamboat or the North River was known by all as Clermont. It was afloat between New York City up the Hudson River to Albany and was operational between 1807 and 1814. The boat was fitted with paddlewheels and a sailing boat and reached speeds of around five miles per hour. It completed the 150-mile journey within 36 hours. It was the very first steamboat to get into service for the public.

The steamboat industry continued to grow however, in 1838 the first fully-fledged steamship, which was designed to become a steamship, dubbed The Great Western, was built by the famous and visionary English engineer Isambard Kingdom Brunel. It was a paddlewheel model that traveled across over the Atlantic carrying passengers. It operated for a period of about ten years before it was the basis for many other steamships of the time. Similar to many early steamships they also had masts and sails that could be utilized in strong wind, or even if the steam engine broke down.

THE AMERICAN INDUSTRIAL REVOLUTION

In some way, Americans were allowed to purchase steam engines from the British but Europeans weren't. But, in any event, Fulton, who had invented the first functioning steamboat was later able to create steamboats with shallow drafts, which traveled both ways along to the Mississippi River. This innovation revolutionized the way that commerce was conducted on this river, making it a 19th-century superhighway.

Prior to the steamboat, traveling against the flow in the river would be challenging, if not unattainable sometimes. Steamboats allowed products as well as passengers were able to be carried in a steady stream.

Steamboats initially used low-pressure Watt design. Later designs utilized a high-pressure system that worked great. About 1810, there were just twenty steamboats operating on the Mississippi River but just 20 years later, there were 1200. The boats were huge but many had an average draft of 4 feet. They were made to carry the molasses, rice, timber, tobacco as well as cotton. Cotton trade was extremely crucial because bales of cotton could be sent through the Mississippi towards New Orleans and then transported up to England that had developed into an enormous marketplace to purchase Southern cotton.

The cotton industry prospered throughout the South because of another Industrial Revolution invention, the Cotton Gin. In 1794, Eli Whitney patented a machine which was able to separate cotton seeds from cotton fiber. This invention enabled cotton farming, and consequent cotton plants very profitable.

The steamboat and cotton gin enabled to the Southern United States to become centres for the cultivation of cotton and, in turn, slavery was very lucrative as well. It was so vital that it was known as King Cotton' since the riches that was accumulated in the South was built on the crop at the end of the 19th century.

Steam engines with high pressure aboard steamboats were the ones which made exporting cotton a possibility. But, they could be extremely risky. Many boiler explosions caused the deaths of 4,000 or more at the time of midcentury. Ships were lit to blaze and then sank, some people also were burned with boiling hot water. One time there was an explosion that which was so strong, it claimed the lives of a few those not in the boat however on the shore. Debris flying from the vessel caused their death.

THE TELEGRAPH AND THE TRANSATLANTIC CABLE

In 1816, the English inventor Francis Ronalds developed the first functioning telephone. His invention was not widely understood in the time and sat for about 20 years before eventually, many of his ideas came into use in the development of commercial telegraphy.

In 1858, the telegraph grown so significant that a transatlantic line between Western Ireland and eastern Newfoundland, Canada was proposed. It was not without issues. The first cable was damaged while the second cable ran for a couple of weeks before it was then broken. In the aftermath of the US Civil War, work was stopped until 1865, when a new cable was laid that also was unsuccessful. However, the project finally reached in 1866. Today, messages could be delivered and picked up within minutes, instead of the 10 days the letter would take to arrive by ships. It was the first time that communication could be established between North America and

Europe and from the beginning of time both continents have been in communications until today.

INVENTORS AND EXPERIMENTERS

At the time, there was a handful of solo inventors that worked on complex technological problems. Most of them unsuccessfully. One of them, Charles Goodyear, spent his whole life trying to solve the challenge in making rubber workable. As he started working on the material, it was instabile. It rotted, or even after treatment, it became hard. Desperate to find the solution and a loss of fortune, he and was living in poverty however, he was determined. He went to the local grocery store carrying the latest concoction of rubber to demonstrate it to his customers. A ball of his material flew from his fingers and fell onto an oven that was boiling hot. As he tried to retrieve it, he thought the temperature would melt the rubber, but however, it burned the rubber before turning into a new material. After he was able to pick it up and looked around, he saw that it was cure. This process of heating, also called vulcanization, was crucial. However, it took additional tests before he could find the precise combination of heat and chemicals required. After he had found it apply for obtained his patent on 1844. In the future, rubber tires would become an essential component in transport since cars, trucks, aircrafts, and bicycles will require rubber tires correctly.

ISAMBARD KINGDOM BRUNEL

As a visionary engineer in the midst of one of most admired Englishmen ever, Isambard Kingdom Brunel could be considered to be a hero figure of the very first Industrial Revolution, the revolution prior to the year 1850.

His works included trains, railways, various ships, tunnels, bridges, even a hospital transportable.

Though many of his plans didn't work out or weren't feasible for the time Brunel's ideas will be the model in the years in the years to come. He was the designer and builder of his Great Britain steamship which was one of the biggest ships at time time. It was built entirely of iron and was driven with propellers, not paddlewheels. This made it an ideal template for future ships. Brunel developed the first idea to create Clifton Suspension Bridge. Clifton Suspension Bridge which had the longest length of any bridge in time time. He also served as an as an assistant engineer in the development of the Thames Tunnel which ran under the Thames River in London and was the first underground tunnel to be constructed beneath an accessible river. Brunel's father served as the main engineer for the project and it utilized Tunneling shield. Tunneling shield that was designed by Brunel's father in order to shield those working on the tunnel from falling over while digging. Brunel also served as the principal engineer of The Great Western Railway which was thought to be one of the greatest achievements in the Victorian Era. The railway line he designed passed through The Box Tunnel, of his concept, which was considered to be the longest railway tunnel of its kind in the world in time time.

THE UGLY SIDE OF THE INDUSTRIAL REVOLUTION

Industrialized nations realized that they had enormous potential. The result was a widespread colonization of Africa up to Asia. Industrial nations can recruit cheap local workers to work on their rubber plantations oil wells, for farming their rice fields and to mine minerals and to cut wood. The resources, or agricultural products of these nations could later be shipped to an industrialized countries where different material and products can be reprocessed and offered for sale at a significant gain. Extermination of indigenous peoples in developing countries was not uncommon until the Second World War. This would not have been feasible on a massive extent prior to it was the Industrial Revolution.

Chapter 4: The 2nd Industrial Revolution

"In the field of science, its primary value is a temporary step-pegged to something greater than. The Principia that Newton in his characteristic modesty titled his masterpiece, really only the beginning of a natural philosophical system as well as not an absolute work as Watt's steam-engine or Arkwright's spinning machine."

Julius Hare

The First Industrial Revolution lasted from around 1760 until approximately the year 1860. The Revolution established the factory system. It was driven through the development of steam engines with many shapes, fabrics, the manufacture of interchangeable pieces and the manufacturing of premium iron.

The Second Industrial Revolution began about in 1860, and ended in 1914, with the beginning in World War One in 1914. It was marked by the development of electricity, the development engine internal combustion which included gasoline as well as Diesel in addition to the manufacture of steel that was high-quality. This was also the time when this revolutionary movement spread across England and was taken up by Germany particularly as well as almost all the other nations across Europe and in the United States and Japan.

Even though being so late in the Industrial Revolution might seem like an advantage, in some ways, it actually was advantageous and advantage, as Germany could prove. The latter half of the 19th Century Germany was beginning to construct factories, melting metal and constructing chemical factories built on the lessons that had was learned. The advanced chemical industry of Germany could benefit from discovering the Periodic Table in 1869 which was the first time recorded and put an outline of the fundamental elements of metal and chemicals that comprised the entirety of the world. Germany didn't have to endure the arduous education curve which England went through in earlier times during the First Industrial Revolution.

Furthermore, a myriad discoveries in science have resulted in a myriad of ideas that seemed almost impossible only a couple of years ago.

For instance, in 1865 James Maxwell formulated the theory of electromagnetic spectrum, that explained how electromagnetic and light waves were viewed as a continuum and that would move through space with an average speed equal to that of light. This idea, later proven, led directly to the knowledge of the radio wave. Marconi used this understanding in order to transmit radio signals greater distances and at higher speeds which culminated in a transatlantic radio transmission in the year 1901.

Historical scholars have pointed out in the early days of the First Revolution, invention led in the right direction and its successes resulted in research in science that resulted in breakthrough discoveries. The new discoveries could, then, result in the development of new technologies. As an example, when James Watt improved the steam engine, thermodynamics laws weren't yet formulated. When they were developed, engineers could take advantages of this information and develop highly advanced devices.

One of the most significant inventions of the 20th century was that of the combustion engine. The inventors were researching this idea since the year 1890 when substantial progress was realized around the year 1860. The year 1884 was when British inventor Edward Butler built the first internal combustion gasoline engine. He by doing this, came up with a host of essential components like the spark plug, magneto, the carburetor as well as the coil ignition. In 1885 Karl Benz made his own engine with four strokes, which he later mounted into the form of an automobile. It was referred to as the Benz Patent-Motorwagen. it was the first vehicle equipped with the internal combustion engine.

Around the time automobile makers were working on their initial plans for cars Two bicycle mechanics tried to take on the difficult task of piloted powered flight. Although a variety of individuals were working on this issue but these two more inexperienced and unfunded youngsters began building gliders with care that later powered planes. Wilbur as well as Orville Wright became icons of The Second Industrial Revolution because they used seat-of-the-pants technology with rigorous observation, measurements and testing in order to develop their models. Furthermore that, when they couldn't locate the perfect internal combustion engine to meet their specific needs, they created one from scratch. They were engineers, scientists and even daredevil pilots. Thus, in 1903, in the cold winter morning that could be dangerous because of snow on the surface, Orville made the first powered flight, in which an aircraft soared up and flies for a brief distance. Although it took years for anyone to appreciate the significance of what they did but they were able to overcome the various difficulties of flying with a pilot and created technical and scientific procedures to allow the plane to develop quickly.

The key to the development of during the Industrial Revolution was workspace and living spaces, particularly in cities that were cramped and had limited spaces to expand. After the huge Chicago Fire in 1871, construction of new structures exploded, but the land for building was swiftly built upon. The architects of 1884 had to reconsider how buildings could be designed.

They created a plan to build high-rise buildings. They relied on brand new steel which has only just been made available. A steel grid skeleton consisting of beams and columns could be constructed to be sturdy enough to withstand the load of windows, floors and the interior. At first, the constructions were usually ten stories high or higher. After some adjustments they could climb to 60 stories. Built in 1912, the Woolworth Building located in New York was 60 stories high, and it is still among the highest buildings across the United States.

It was another vital technology that made the possibility of tall buildings feasible and that was the development of the safe elevator. Although elevators have been in use for quite some time but the first safe elevator was invented by Elisha Graves Otis. The elevator was operated by steam engine. At the beginning in the 19th century elevators had been operated by electric motors. the tall building could be considered a viable style.

THE UNITED STATES

In 1869, within the United States, the first Transcontinental Railroad as it was known, was built. The line, which ran for 1,912 miles, been built from an old track that ran from the east and terminated in Iowa. The brand new track was constructed up to the Pacific coast, in San Francisco. The rail line was now running starting from New York straight through to San Francisco. In 1876, an express train named"the Transcontinental Express made the journey within 84 hours, which was about three and a half days. The same area that pioneers who had covered wagons travelled when they traveled towards west coast. West Coast, which had earlier took three months or longer.

Chapter 5: The Consumer Society

"Some of my readers who are young have amazing imaginations. I am delighted by this. Imagined thinking has helped mankind progress from into the Dark Ages to its present level of civilisation. The power of imagination was the catalyst that led Columbus to find America. It was imagining that was the catalyst that led Franklin to find electricity. It was the imagination that gave us steam engines and the telephone as well as the talking machine, and even the automobile. These objects had to be dreamed of before becoming reality. Thus, my belief is that the dreams of a day -- fantasies that you can't help but look at them with eyes open and your brain's machine whirling bring about the good of humanity. Children who are imaginative will be the creative person who is most likely to invent the world, invent, and thus to help build a better civilisation. An experienced teacher tells that stories from fairytales have immense value for creating imagination in children. I agree with it."

L. Frank Baum

Although many people struggled to make ends meet and work long work hours, many advantages brought about by the Industrial Revolution began to improve everyday life for people of all ages. By the time of Second Industrial Revolution in 1914 how people did their work, lived and even played was completely different from what they were doing the same things 100 years prior.

One of the most notable inventions was the electrical light invented created by Thomas Edison. The light bulb Edison invented lasted for 1200 hours, and was two times more efficient than gas lighting, and five times more efficient than lighting with kerosene - both which were used in the beginning of Industrial Revolution. A good light source meant that one could sit and read in the evening or wander around the city after dark. Amusement Parks such as Coney Island in New York City showcased their brilliant lights against the dark and dreary city during the same time to provide a great location to visit after work.

Many consumer items designed for home use that were high-quality and affordable began to become accessible, like Ivory Soap produced from Procter & Gamble, Kellogg's Corn Flakes, Fig Newtons and Oreo Cookies by Nabisco, as well as Coca-Cola as well as tea bags. Canned food products, which had developed around 1810, was now a huge industry and food items that were cheap could remain in storage for months, without getting spoiled.

In the wake of the introduction of electric lighting and electric service for most houses the new electrical devices were developed and then widely distributed including the vacuum cleaner washer, toaster and the waffle iron. the refrigerator, as well as the air cooling.

Another electronic gadget called a telephone would soon be a in every home that allows instant voice calls at any time from any residence or office in the United States to any other residence or company.

The industry of textiles began with the Industrial Revolution, was by the time it was highly developed and offered the entire range of ready-to wear clothes at a reasonable cost even though wealthy customers could still afford to buy custom-made clothes. Furthermore to that, it was the Singer sewing machine was extremely popular with women who wanted to sew clothes themselves.

One of the most fascinating development there were a variety of entertainment-related products were created that were then upgraded year after year.

Movies and films were popular. Instead of spending around 100 dollars to buy an Broadway tickets for New York, for example people could view movies for less than 2 dollars, which is a bargain in the present. Phonographs were invented as well as the disc record recordings offered entertainment for the masses that could be enjoyed by a vast number of people.

Newspapers were also very popular. Printing technology advancements reduced the cost of printing however they also enabled a variety of versions to be released within a single day. Furthermore to this, the recently developed halftone technique meant that photos were now included too. The cost of newspapers was as low as 1 cent (a quarter of a dollar today). They became so popular that it was estimated that there two issues of newspapers printed to each individual within the United States every day.

Photography, which begun to be invented during the first half of 1800, was also a popular choice. From the early 19th century it was still practiced by experts who employed big format cameras, individual pieces of film, and also created their own negatives and prints. George Eastman changed all that through the creation of a camera, he named the Brownie that used a flexible film that could take many pictures onto the roll. The name of his company was "You Click the Button and We do the rest." In the beginning, people purchased the camera, then took photographs in bright sunlight outside, then took their camera to Kodak for unloading and to develop the films and prints. The marketing method was extremely popular and people soon wanted to own a Kodak camera to capture the activities of their families and create an album of the family.

The bicycle of the present was invented and built. It was regarded as the first bike of this type, The Rover, had two wheels of the same dimensions, a chain which drove the rear wheel as well as air-filled tires. The bicycle gained a lot of popularity and, to this day, there are more bicycles than automobiles all over the globe.

Beginning in 1892, a business from the United States named Sears and Roebuck created a mail-order catalog which first offered watches and jewellery. It soon expanded to cover everything you could possibly find at an hardware or department store. The catalog made use of the huge rail system in place so products could be easily transported. The catalog was a way for any person within the United States could buy these low-cost consumer products regardless of where they resided. In that time the majority of people resided in the United States, which meant this catalog was able to reach a completely different class of customers.

Perhaps the most significant achievement in the field of consumer goods was a low-cost car that was reliable and was able to handle the rough roads that were common at the time. Within the United States, Henry Ford worked on building an automobile of this kind. While he constructed and designed the cars, he assigned each one an alphabetical designation. But he didn't make all the cars since they were all prototypes. The first model was an Model A and the next was a Model B, but it was not until he got the letters T that he realized that he could have the perfect combination of a sturdy, inexpensive vehicle that was able to be quickly and swiftly assembled. It was called The Model T. The Model T is regarded as the first automobile that was mass produced and there was more than sixteen million cars sold. The first time it was offered for sale in 1908, and continued still in production up to 1927.

"I I will design a car to serve the vast majority. It'll be spacious enough to be able to house the whole family yet small enough for an driver to operate and take care of. It'll be made using the highest quality materials by the top men to be found, following the most basic designs technology can create. It will also cost so little that any person earning an income of a decent amount can afford to buy one and share with his loved ones the joy of endless enjoyment within God's beautiful space."

Henry Ford

Ford was not just the first to have created and constructed a car which everyone could afford, but he also invented an assembly line that drastically reduced the cost and increased production. This model would later be replicated in a myriad of industries as Ford demonstrated the possibility that a complex system like the car could be produced in mass quantities. His innovations paved towards mass production.

The other advances were too.

Andrew Carnegie was a poor Scottish immigrants who came into America as a child. United States as a boy. In the course of his life, he built up a massive fortune mostly through the production of steel. He was at one point the richest man within America. United States. After his retirement, and decided to donate the bulk of his wealth to support the advancement of science, education, and peace around the world. For the average person the biggest contribution was the creation of 3000 libraries in the United States, Canada, as well as others English spoken nations. He donated around 95% of his money. Libraries that were free became safe havens as well as centers for those looking to further their education.

There was one last improvement that could create an enormous difference to the lives of ordinary citizens - the creation of parks that are accessible to all.

In 1873, Central Park in New York City was opened for public use. Central Park was considered to be an area for everyone starting from the smallest factory worker to the top executive at a company; it was a space that "all could be welcomed regardless of wealth or rank." This was considered to be a revolutionary concept during the time. It was planned in the hands of Frederick Law Olmsted. Olmsted wanted the park to be spacious, relaxing and an area in which New Yorkers could be far from the bustle and noise of the city. The city that is now a significant component during the Industrial Revolution. Many consider the park as one of the most beautiful pieces of artwork created in that time. The creation of the park was so simple, many believed that Olmsted was not doing anything to create it. Actually, 4 million plants were added and over ten million dirt carts had been cleared. Olmsted's designs would later become an example for similar parks. In the end it was possible to find a variety of parks that carried similar messages of welcome throughout across the United States.

Chapter 6: The Industrial Society

"I was among the worst-hit provinces in Turkey But never, under the most obscene of corrupt governments have I witnessed such deplorable miserable conditions as I've witnessed after my return to the very midst of an Christian country."

The speaker was Lord Byron who delivered an address before Lord Byron, in a speech to the House of Lords in England on the 27th of February, 1812.

The revolutionary shift in the power generation process which was brought about by steam engines and the creation of massive factories marked the start of the Industrial Revolution, but it also marked a radical change in how society was constructed and constituted.

Prior to the factory system in the past, a decentralized and individual production of products, also known in the system of home was still in operation. The domestic system was a place where people worked in their homes or in workshop. They had their own equipment they set their own working hours and were spread across the country.

The factory's system was a complete change of this. The workers now worked for factories that provided machines and instructed them on which days to be at work. The factories were situated near the main roads or waterways initially to ensure that huge quantities of merchandise could be transported to them for processing, and they could deliver the final product. The factories later on could be situated in various areas due to the steam engine, but they were always near railroad routes for receiving and transferring produced items.

The result was that a lot of residents who lived in the countryside were living in cramped houses in cities and towns in close proximity to factories. It was a low-paying job as well as the facilities were not clean and safe as well as properly illuminated.

Furthermore, the majority jobs didn't necessitate skilled labour. The result was that highly skilled males typically could not get jobs since women earning lesser and had children paying even less were being employed to perform the job.

The factory's new system of production was not without its own consequences. As the industry grew into manufacturing in mass, the parts were interchangeable. Before this, craftsmen created individual components specifically for specific rifles, for instance. Now, one piece could be used to replace a similar part for a rifle line. The result was that the workers were no longer needed and were forced to working in factories where wages were low, and their talents were not needed.

Though no one was planning the current situation England specifically was a nation where the workers endured a life of poverty and sickly and caused workers' protests.

There were two major movements designed to stop the development of the industrial system, or to give workers greater rights.

The initial movement was known in the early days as Luddites. These were mostly experienced weavers opposed to the invention of machine-woven weaving that made some of their techniques outdated. Some of their activities became violent, and at various moments British soldiers were instructed to fight the Luddites. In one instance, there were more troops fighting Luddites than British soldiers. Luddites than British troops fighting Napoleon's army Spain.

The Luddite movement was first introduced in 1811, and ended five years following. At the time factories were targeted machines were destroyed, and the owners and managers of the mills were executed. In 1813, a group of Luddites were tried in connection with their rebellious actions. Seventeen were hanged. The purpose of this was to show the way as it was to ensure justice. Additionally that the destruction of machines was made a crime of capital punishment and a person may be convicted of murder and receive the penalty for destruction of factories' property. Following these draconian measures then, the Luddite trend waned however, the anger remained to grow and grew worse. It would eventually come out in different types.

There was for a long time an associated movement for unionization of the workforce. Workers were protesting against working long hours, low wages and poor working conditions. In 1799, the federal government adopted the Combination Act which made such organization illegal, and also made Unions unconstitutional. Then, in 1824 when it was clear that working class had continued to form and join Unions which was legalized by the government, they reformed Trade Unions. It was just the beginning but it was also the beginning of a lengthy struggle between employees and the owners of factories that was not resolved for over a century.

There was also horrible working conditions as well as child abuse working in factories. The initial Factory Act was passed by the government, which restricted the employment of children within the textile industry only to those who were over nine, and also set couple of conditions for kids with a higher age. In particular, kids aged 14-18 could not be working longer than 12 hours in a day, while children aged 9-13 were able to only be employed for eight hours per each day. Although this was a beginning, it was only to deal with a problem which had started about 70 years prior. Additionally, it didn't restrict the industry of coal that employed children extensively due to their small size and had the ability to travel in places that adults could not.

In 1842, the Mines Act was passed which made it illegal for children to be under 10 from being employed in mines for coal. In the past, children who were as young as old worked in moist mines that were filled with dust from coal. The terrible conditions were neglected for years since England has become an international superpower powered by coal, and it was also the case that coal was plentiful on that island. The English wanted to not stop the mining industry, however the way children were treated meant the need for something to be addressed.

The coal mines prospered and coal became the primary energy source for the rise of England's power. Steam engines were powered with coal, as did metal foundries. Steel and iron became the main material in that time. In 1800, ten million tonnes of coal had been mined each year. The mining increased by decade, until by 1900 more than two hundred million tonnes of coal had been mined.

The consequences of this Revolution in addition. After you consider that Industrial Revolution had completely taken over, it altered the people's perception of time and the way they viewed time. Railroads were run on strict times, as an example. In the end, in order to eliminate confusion, the railroads decided to insist on fixed time zones rather than the local times each town used for a number of hundreds of years. The time zones were tied to the hour of high noon in the respective locations. Each mile of longitude had the exact time. Instead of sunrise or sunset on the sun's setting, industrial facilities will decide when workers would be working and would have them clock in and out.

The move to cities, of people who grew up in rural village and agricultural areas, created its own issues. In the cities, the tight connection people shared with the country had disappeared. Therefore, crime and illegal activity increased. The 1829 Peel's Metropolitan Police Act was enacted to set up the first ever professional police. It was known by the name of Metropolitan Police it oversaw the Greater London zone.

While this major social reorganization was taking over, several Social and political groups were beginning to emerge. There were uprisings and protests across all countries of Europe which had gotten industrialized. The protests were brutally repressed and at the exact time the pamphlet that was not widely known was released titled The Manifesto of the Communist Party by Karl Marx as well as Friedrich Engels. They dreamed of an industrial society that wasn't owned by elites but owned by workers. They were certain the possibility of a revolution within England or another developed nation would be the very first country to embrace their vision. But it was actually an agricultural-based country that had little industry Russia was the first nation to adopt their idea into practice.

In the year 1900, governments began to realize that factories couldn't be allowed to offer items to the general public without control. One of the most dramatic instances, Upton Sinclair's novel The Jungle detailed the soiled environment of the meat processing production industry in Chicago. The same year the book was released, The Federal Meat Inspection Act of 1906 (FMIA) was approved by the United States. This law provided penalties for labeling meat incorrectly and legislated hygiene standards within the meat production facilities.

Chapter 7: War And Peace In The Future

Anthem for Doomed Youth

What bells do they have for those who pass away in the cattle industry?

The only thing that can stop them is the sheer gun's fury.

The only exception is the rifle's stuttering fast rattle

Are able to twirl their messy orisons.

They are not laughing now No bells or prayers;

There is no mourning voice except the choirs.--

The loud, demented choruses of screaming shells

They're calling bugles from the sad shires.

Which candles could be lit for speeding them up?

They are not the ones who control boys, but rather in their the eyes of their

Shall shine with the holy sparkles of the end.

The blush of women's eyebrows will be the pale;

Their blossoms show the gentleness of a patient mind,

Each dusk slows down, the blinds are drawn down.

The poem was written by Wilfred Owen, a soldier from World War One who was murdered just prior to the close of the conflict.

In 1862, on March 8-9 The US Civil War naval battle in Hampton Roads was so dramatic and decisive that it radically changed how warships were constructed in the years following. This was the first naval battle of ironclad ships. Two steam-powered ironclad vessels such as that of the Southern Confederacy's Merrimack and the

Monitor of the Union Monitor demonstrated that the future belonged to ships that were covered in iron plates or constructed of iron. The Merrimack was able to sink two massive wooden Union vessels before the Monitor was launched the following day. The Confederate vessel was so powerful that it was threatening to destroy the Union blockade that had been held the South. On the 9th of March, both on March 9, Monitor along with the Merrimack were at war, however there was no winner clear.

However, it was evident that warships made of wood were an outdated notion. The famous battle on the sea could only be a preview of how warfare would become more modernized by the Industrial Revolution.

The Industrial Revolutions of the past two centuries had significant changes to combat, yet they were not widely known and was not recognized until civil war was declared.

Europe has been at peaceful, at least for the major time, following the fall of Napoleon in 1815. The majority of people were of the opinion that this peace would be maintained. In addition, the monarchs of Europe considered themselves to have an absolute control over their respective countries, and believed those who were displeased with their work force were in the best case, a nuisance.

The whole thing exploded the fateful day that archduke Ferdinand from Austria was murdered in Serbia on the 28th of June 1914. The carefully planned alliances meant to stop war broke down and in the end, the largest European powerhouses declared the war. The problem was that few knew the war would be an entirely distinct war, one unlike anything that has ever been waged. This would be the first battle in which arsenals created during the Industrial Revolution would mechanize the deaths of millions. Thus, for instance there would be tens or thousands of soldiers would be killed within a day just for a couple of inches of land. It was also known throughout Europe by the name of The Great War.

The number of guns available was awe-inspiring. Machine guns were able to kill troops just like harvesting machines could chop through rows of corn the field. Barbed wire made advancement across open ground almost impossible. Railroads could quickly transport troops for any advance by the enemy. High explosives, or as they were referred to during the Great War, also known as shrapnel shells were extremely deadly. They exploded above the battlefield, and later sprayed shrapnel that was deadly down on the soldiers who were advancing. Furthermore, Germany, in particular has made usage of its sophisticated chemical industry as well as chemical weapons. The numerous improvements made to the rifles of soldiers meant they could have a precise range that was more than one mile. They could be fired and reloaded quickly, and due to the interchangeable components they were quickly repaired on the spot. Submarines played an equally important function. Airplanes were also employed but their full potential was not realized until after in the Second World War.

There was more. The Crowned Chiefs of Europe were relying on expert soldiers to wage war. Today, nations rely on ordinary citizens to fight. In the war, countries adopted conscription law that required young men to join the military.

The seemingly altruistic education public that the majority of European nations had started to provide to their children additionally meant that these previous pupils would soon be good soldiers. The 1880 English Education Act required all kids aged 10 or less in age to go to schools. The children were able to study rather than being required to perform work at an extremely young age. Then, a later

Education Act would raise the minimum age to 14. Although this may seem like a noble gesture and indeed it was but there was a more sinister motive at work here. Every one of the European governments knew that in any future wars, they'd need to recruit citizens into the fight. Children who were educated by their country were able to accept orders from officers in the same way like students who had received orders from their instructors. That's what was happening during World War One and World War Two.

The defense planners likely had a contingency plan which they anticipated would need the conscription of ordinary men to fight in the war and that with a public education system, the soldiers would be better able to manage in their military forces, they didn't think that there might have to be major changes that they did not anticipate. The millions of people that were compelled to serve now demanded an increased voice in administration; they demanded greater freedom of speech. In the end, when the monarchs of Europe took part in conflicts, they also opened the way to greater participation of their own citizens. The citizens believed that if they were required to fight it was time for the government to provide them with a greater the chance to speak.

This is exactly what took place. At the close of the 20th Century democratic laws and a system of government which protected the rights of the workers were in all of Europe and in many other countries also. The majority of the royals of Europe weren't in the position of power.

FUTURE CONSEQUENCES

Two extremely difficult issues must be resolved now that our Industrial Revolution has a firm influence on almost all societies and nations around the world.

Industrialization's end-products can be blamed for a large part of the what scientists call global warming, or climate change. The technology needs to be controlled and developed so that it doesn't harm the environment like it has in the past fifty years. Additionally, the garbage generated by different products like plastic bags, and other plastic items which pollute the oceans, also needs to be dealt with.

We are now facing the toughest issue of population growth. Within a matter of a couple of years, according to some estimates in 2050, the planet will be able to support the highest amount of people it is capable of supporting. However, it is highly unlikely the increase in human population will slow down to a point. There's no simple solution to the issue, however the solution must be discovered. Certain studies have proven that when the majority of people have what is essential to live a healthy and safe life, they are able to are more likely to have children would then be encouraged to attend schools and be educated. It could be the best way to address the issue.

TODAY'S INDUSTRIAL REVOLUTION

Our world now is the one built through the Industrial Revolution. Actually, we're on the other side of technological revolution, thanks to computers as well as the Internet. Our lifestyle and the towns we reside in and the goods we purchase as well as the job we are employed on are all part this phase of the Industrial Revolution.

Nowadays, we lead more healthy and longer lives than the people who lived at the time of Industrial Revolution and we also face threats from nuclear weapons that could destroy a whole city within a few minutes.

And unlike many of the historical narratives which seem distant the revolution that is taking place today is taking place and it will affect your personal life, in large part in the present.

"It is possible to argue that humanity has gained from the advancement of technology over steam engines. Electricity offers endless conveniences for ever increasing number of people, though they might be forced to pay a high price to enjoy them. In my thinking, however, I am unable to think about the combustion engine inside that created the planet even smaller. More importantly, we must be wary of what the consequences will be of giving humans who are so marginally distinct from the predecessors in the so-called barbarous times with such horrible agencies like the nuclear bomb. Please give me a horse."

Chapter 8: The Timeline And The Changes That Occurred In The Industrial Revolution

The Industrial Revolution was a period of change that took place in Britain and the continent of Europe as well as in the USA between 1760 and around 1820 and 1840 when the introduction of new manufacturing techniques. A shift away from hand-to devices, a new kind of manufacturing strategies for iron and chemical and the increased usage of waterpower and steam, the development of machine tools and the rise of a mechanized manufacturing system are all aspects of this shift. In the course of this change, Industrial Revolution also introduced a time of astonishing expansion of the population.

Concerning work, output, and investment capital, the textiles were the primary market during all of the Industrial Revolution. The textiles industry was also among the first market segments to implement new production techniques.

The Industrial Revolution started in the U.K., and a majority of the technological and design innovations were created in Britain.

With the help that were carried out by the East India Company, Britain was the leading industrial country in the late 18th century. The country controlled a world-wide trading empire that included groups from The USA and Canada and the Caribbean as well as a significant influence over the military and politics in the Indian subcontinent, particularly in the early industrialized Mughal Bengal.

One of the primary factors that led to that Industrial Revolution was the development of commerce and the growth of businesses.

In which region the revolution introduced all its transformations, as well as the implications this brought to children, families as well as the farmers' economy and the politics.

The Industrial Revolution was a watershed period in human history that impacted every aspect of our lives in a way. Average salaries and populations, particularly, began expanding at an unparalleled speed. Many financial experts say that the primary effect from the Industrial Revolution was that the overall standard of living throughout the world began increasing often for the very first time ever in the history of mankind, whereas other experts say that it did not begin to increase in significance until in the 19th and beginning of the twentieth century.

Prior to the Industrial Revolution and the creation of the current capitalist economic system GDP per capita remained relatively stable, and it was the Industrial Revolution introduced an age of financial per-capita development in capitalist societies.

According to the financial historians that the beginning of the Industrial Revolution was the most significant event in the history of mankind prior to the introduction of domestic animals and plants.

The historians are divided on the exact date that they believe the Industrial Revolution started and ended and also the pace that social and financial transformations occurred.

The Industrial Revolution started in Britain during the 1780s, and was not evident until in the 1830s and 1840s According to the Eric Hobsbawm however T. S. Ashton was adamant that it occurred between 1760-1830. Rapid industrialization began in Britain around 1780, with mechanical spinning. It was then rapid growth of steam power and the production of iron about 1800. The early 19th century, mechanized textile production spread away from Great Britain to continental Europe and to the United States, with big iron, textile, coal, and steam centers emerging in Belgium and in the United States, and consequently textiles were produced in France.

The use of early Industrial Revolution innovations, such as automated spinning and weaving stagnated and the markets for them developed between the end of 1830s until the beginning of 1840s. This led to a recession in the financial market. The late-period advancements, for instance the widespread use of steamboats and engines and steamships as well as hot blast iron melting, as well as modern innovations, such as the telegraph with electrical power, which were widely introduced between the 1840s-1850s did not have enough power to produce large development rates. Following 1870, an explosive growing financial markets began due to a brand new collection of developments referred to by the term 2nd Industrial Revolution. Modern methods for making steel, mass production assemblies lines, electric grid systems, large machine tool manufacturing, and working with progressively advanced inventions within steam-powered factories were just a few of innovations.

Beginning in the second half in the 1800s there were a few developments that directly relate with the start in the Industrial Revolution. In the early 1830s, major breakthroughs in technology had taken place through the following areas:

Textilesusing steam or water-powered mechanical spinning increased the productivity of an employee by a factor of 500. The power loom increased employees' production in a way that was more than 40. In the case of cotton, gin production increased by 50 percent when it was time to draw the seeds out of cotton. The spinning of linen and wool as well as weaving witnessed significant improvements in effectiveness, however not exactly to the similar degree to cotton.

Steam power-The efficiency of steam engines was increased until they utilized one-fifth or one-tenth in fuel. Steam engines that were fixed could be adjusted to move rotary, which made suitable for commercial use. Because of their high power-to-weight ratio, this high-pressure engine was suited for transportation. The steam engine was introduced in 1800 and was a major rise.

Production of iron - the use of charcoal instead of coke significantly reduced the price of making wrought iron as well as pig iron. the production of iron.

Coke was able to power larger blast heating equipment, which resulted the most cost-effective blast heating systems. The mid-1750s saw steam engines were the first to be employed to drive blasting air (indirectly through pumping water onto an waterwheel) which allowed for a significant growth in iron production eliminating the limitations that water powered power had.

Around 1760, the first iron blowing cylinder came into use. It was later improved by adding double operating, allowing the blast heating system to be heated at higher levels. For a much lower price that the finery generates the method of puddling created high-quality structural iron. It took fifteen times more time to make wrought iron roll than hammer it. Over the years after, it was discovered that the blast hot (1828) significantly improved the performance of the iron's fuel production.

Maker tools are invented.the first tools for devices are invented. The screw-cutting lathe, cylindrical dull device, as well as the milling machine were among these. Although it took a while to develop efficient processes the device tools have enabled the efficient production of precision metallic parts.

Chapter 9: Broken Down Per Market

We'll look at some of the most innovative innovations that have been made at this time of the year and breakdown them into smaller pieces and classify them by market.

Fabric Production

The year 1750 was the one in which in 1750, the U.K. imported 2.5 million pounds of cotton in raw form of which a large portion was spun and weaved in Lancashire's local market. Work was performed at hand, in the homes of employees or, on more unusual occasions, at the shops of master weaver. The year 1787 saw 22 million lbs of raw cotton was gathered Many of which were washed to remove dirt, shredded, and spun with machines.

The consumption of cotton on the British textile market increased to 52 million pounds in year 1800 and reached 588 million pounds during the 1850 year.

The cotton fabrics have a long time in the regions in India, China, Central America, South America, as well as the Middle East, and they were a very popular market in the year 1000 AD. The majority of them were made by tiny farmers with their crops for food in subtropical and tropical environments which was then weaved and spun by families mostly for use in domestic homes. China began to require homes to pay some of their tax obligations in cotton around the fifteenth century. The majority of Chinese wear cotton clothing until the end of 17th century. The material could be utilized as legal tender virtually anyplace. The production of cotton fabrics was in huge quantities to export markets in India generally by expert weaver. Weaving workshops of varying sizes were run by entrepreneurs. India made a wide range of cotton fabrics and some had a high-quality.

Prior to its use on plantations owned by colonists in the Americas it was a difficult substance to Europe to obtain.

Native Americans have been found to produce two yet to be discovered varieties of premium quality cotton: sea-isle cotton (Gossypium barbadense) and the upland the green-seeded variety (Gossypium hirsutum) from the time of early Spanish the explorers. Sea isle cotton was a common crop in tropical regions, specifically along Georgia and the barrier islands of South Carolina, but was unable to make it through the time in the inland. Barbados started exporting sea-isle cotton in the year 1650. The green seeded cotton was a success in the inland areas in the south United States, but it was not successful because of the difficulties in the removal of seeds that was overcome by cotton Gin. A strain of cotton seeds that was brought over from Mexico into Natchez, Mississippi in the year 1806 became the hereditary base for nearly 90%

of the world's production of cotton today. It produces up to 4 times faster selecting bolls.

The flying shuttle bus created in 1733, by John Kay and enhanced and every year since, which also included one in 1747 that doubled the weaver's productivity, increasing the unevenness between weaving and spinning. A son of John's, Robert, developed the dropbox that helped make changing the color of thread much easier. It was widely used by the people of Lancashire in the years following 1760.

The frame for spinning rollers and the flyer-and-bobbin device for pulling wool towards a higher density were created through Lewis Paul. John Wyatt of Birmingham helped in the development of the technique. Paul Wyatt and Paul Wyatt started the mill in Birmingham using their inventive donkey-powered rolling machines. The year 1743 saw the factory of Northampton began operation with five Paul and Wyatt machines, each equipped with 50 spindles.

It was operational until about 1764. Daniel Bourn set up a similar mill in Leominster and it eventually burned down. The year 1748 saw Lewis Paul and Daniel Bourn each registered carding devices. The device was later utilized in the very first device for spinning cotton which was based on two sets of rolling wheels that were moving at distinct speed. Richard Arkwright's waterframe and Samuel Crompton's spinning mule further improvements on Lewis's idea.

James Hargreaves created the spinning jenny in Stanhill, Lancashire, in 1764. He patent it in 1770. It was the first practical spindle with multiple spinning wheels. The jenny operated similarly like a spinning wheel by securing the fibers, before pulling them out, and then turning the fibers. It was a simple wooden frame with 40 spindles which was priced at L 6 in 1792. The jenny was mostly used by spinners at home. The jenny spun delicately twisting yarn that was only used to make weft and not as a warp.

Richard Arkwright developed the spinning frame, commonly called the water frame. He patent it in 1769, along with two other co-workers. The concept was influenced partially by a spinning device designed specifically for Thomas High by clockmaker John Kay the same person Arkwright was using. The water frame sucked up the fiber. It was then turned through the spindle by employing a succession of four sets of rollers. Each moving at a higher speed than the last one. The fiber's length was more than the space between rollers.

The fibers split due to spacing that was not sufficient and the thread became unsteady when it was distant. The top rollers were leather covered as well as a weight utilized to transfer an electric force to push the rollers. The weights prevented the twist from reversed ahead and behind the rolling wheels. The lower rollers were made out of steel and wood and were fitted with fluting that ran throughout their length. The water frame was able to have the capability of producing an elastic, medium-count warp thread. This allowed Britain to create a 100 cotton-based fabric in the very first time. The first manufacturing facility to utilize this spinning machine was run by horses. It was named after Arkwright and his colleagues using water-powered machines in a plant situated in Cromford, Derbyshire, in the year 1771.

Wool.

The first automated process of spinning in Europe however it was much more difficult to automatize that cotton spin. Efficiency of spinning wool increased dramatically in the course of the Industrial Revolution, though not quite as high as that of cotton.

Silk.

John Lombe's steam-powered silk mill located in Derby that was operational until

1721, could be the first fully mechanised market. Lombe discovered how to create silk thread while working as a spies for the commercial market in Italy but, just since the Italian silk market remained afloat and its secrets well-guarded what was the status of the industry during the time remains a mystery. Silk raw materials from Italy was stopped in order to eliminate competitors, despite being aware that Lombe's facility proved to be technically efficient. The Crown provided the production models from Lombe's plant to be displayed in the Tower of London to stimulate production.

The markets for steel and iron.

Bar iron was one of the most common sort of iron utilized to fabricate hardware, such as nail, wire, hinges and horseshoes. It also made wagon tires chains, geometric shapes and designs. Steel was produced out of a tiny amount bar iron. Cast iron was utilized to make pots, ranges and many other applications in which the brittleness of cast iron was able to withstand. The majority of it was improved and then transformed into bar iron, which led to massive loss. The bloomery method that was the most popular method of smelting iron until the latter part of the 18th century could also be used to create bar iron.

Iron Process Improvements.

The substitution of biofuels and wood by coal represented a major transformation in the iron industry during time time that was the Industrial Revolution. Mining coal required lesser labor to produce a certain amount of heat, compared to making wood into a combustible form and then converting into charcoal. Furthermore, coal was more readily available than wood, which was rare prior to the end of the 1800s's huge increase in iron production.

The year 1750 saw the first time that coke predominantly changed the charcoal used in smelting process of copper and lead and was also employed to make glass. Due to the high sulfur content in coal, it made less iron during the refining and smelting of iron, as opposed to charcoal. Although low sulfur coals were recognized but they contained dangerous levels of sulfur. The sulfur level in coal can be reduced by the conversion to coke. Only a small portion of coals is coking.

The lack of power from water to power blast bellows was a further limitation restricting the iron industry prior up to Industrial Revolution. The steam engine was able to overcome this limitation. power to break through this restriction.

The use of coal for iron smelting prior to when it became the Industrial Revolution, thanks to innovations made of Sir Clement Clerke and associates in 1678. The team employed reverberatory heating methods using coal that were referred to as cupolas. The fires worked on the ore, charcoal, or coke mix, which transformed the oxide into metal that's the way they operated. This has the advantage in preventing pollution (such such as sulphurash) from transferring into the material. This method was first used on lead around 1678 and later for copper, in 1687. It was in the 1690s that it was used also in iron foundries. However the refresitory heater was referred to as a heater for air. (The foundry cupola, however, on its own, is an added feature later).

The Power of Steam.

The development of the steam engine fixed was an important component in the Industrial Revolution; however, most of the commercial power supply was generated via wind and water in the initial phases of this revolution. In 1800, steam had provided approximately ten thousand horses power across the UK. Steam power has climbed up to 210,000 horses power up to 1815.

Thomas Savery, in the 1698 was the first commercial steam-powered machine.

Savery invented and developed an low-lift mix vacuum high pressure water pumps in London which produced around one horsepower (hp) as well as was employed in a few water sources and numerous mining operations (therefore that it became the "brand," The Miner's Good Friend). When it came to smaller horsepower versions it was inexpensive and durable, however in larger capacities it could be vulnerable to blasts of boiler. Pumps from Savery were manufactured up to the latter part of the 18th century.

Thomas Newcomen introduced the first efficient piston steam engine prior to 1712. In Britain there were a few Newcomen engines were constructed for draining pipes, which were previously considered unpractical deep mines. The engine was located on the surface They were massive machines which cost lots of money to develop and could produce as much as 3.5 5 kW. (5 hp). Pumps used for the community water system were as well operated by these. These were not properly handled by modern standards however, because they were located close to coal mines, which was not expensive pits, they let mines to be deeper and allowed the coal mining industry to expand dramatically.

Tools for Devices.

Millwrights built windmills and watermills and carpenters made frame for the lumber industry, and turners and smiths constructed steel pieces to make pre-industrial machines. Joints of all kinds tend to be able to rack (work loose) as they grew with time and the wood pieces could be a problem because they changed the measurements based on temperature and humidity. Machines that used metal parts and frames were more common in the course of time as they developed as the Industrial Revolution developed. Metal components were also utilized in the manufacture of weapons and threaded fasteners, such as bolts for devices, screws, and nuts. Also, accuracy was required in the production of components. Accuracy could allow for more efficient working equipment, parts interchangeability as well as threaded fastener in harmony.

The requirement for parts made of metal led to the development of specific gadgets. They were developed around the turn of the century, by clockmakers and watchmakers and even by home-based instruments for clinical makers, in order to allow their users to make mini gadgets in bulk.

The production of metal was done by hand prior to the invention of machine tools. They used hammers scrapers, files, saws and chisels to be the typical hand instruments. In the following years, the use of device components made from metal was decreased. The production process was time-consuming expensive, and accurate was difficult to achieve.

A cylinder dull tool developed by John Wilkinson in the year 1774, was the very first important accuracy device. It was utilized to bore steam engines of the early days large-diameter cylindrical cylinders. The cutting device used by Wilkinson's dull tool was mounted on a wood beam that ran through the cylinder that was tired and was supported by a pillar from both ends as unlike the earlier cantilevered systems that were used to bore dull cannon.

In the beginning of the 19th century the planing device and milling device as well as the making device were invented. Even though it is true that milling devices were designed at the same time but it was not created as a real workshop instrument until later in the 19th century.

Henry Maudslay, a dazzling mechanic working for the Royal Arsenal, Woolwich, created a school for maker of device tools in the 19th century in the early years. He worked as an apprentice in Jan

Verbruggen's Royal Weapon Foundry. Jan Verbruggen set up a horizontal dulling device in Woolwich in 1774. It was the first UK commercial-sized lathe. Joseph Bramah appointed Maudslay to create high-security locks made of metal that required meticulous workmanship. Lathes similar to mover rest lathe was invented by Bramah.

Maudslay invented the lathe that slides that used interchangeable components between the spindle and lead screw for cutting device screws of different thread pitches. Screws were not made with precision before development using different earlier designs for lathes, some that were reconstructed using a design model.

One of the greatest inventions was the mover rest lathe. Even though it was clear that it was not entirely the idea of Maudslay, Maudslay was the first to create a functioning lathe made of a combination of well acknowledged innovations such as the slide rest, the lead screw as well as change machines.

Maudslay quit Bramah's work and started his own business. At his time at the Portsmouth Block Mills, he was hired to construct machines to manufacture block sheaves for ships to the Royal Navy. These all-metal machines were the first ones to be utilized in mass production as well as making interchangeable parts. Maudslay applied the knowledge that he learned regarding the necessity for accuracy and stability in the development of devices, and also in his workshops the man taught generations of men that included Richard Roberts, Joseph Clement as well as Joseph Whitworth, to continue the work he had begun.

The first three quarters of the century James Fox of Derby and Matthew Murray of Leeds both were able to use devices in a growing export trade. Roberts was an innovator in the field of using evaluations and jigs for precision measuring workshop measurements and also a maker of high-end device equipment.

Tools for the device had limited influence during their peak at the time in the Industrial Revolution since there were only a few metal items that were mass-produced apart from threaded fasteners, weapons along with a host of other items. Methods for mass-producing metal products that are accurate enough for interchangeability generally credited to a project that was part of the US Department of War that developed interchangeable gun parts at the beginning of the 19th century.

The market for devices increased to become the most lucrative commercial part that is part of the U.S. economy by value and was viewed as a result of the discovery of essential tool for devices.

Chemicals

In the course of throughout the Industrial Revolution, massive chemical production was an enormous leap forward. The lead chamber method that was invented through Englishman John Roebuck (James Watt's first collaborator) in 1746, was the very first to create sulphuric acid. Through replacing the costly glass vessels with larger chambers, which were cheaper to build with lead slammed together it was possible to dramatically increase the size of production. Instead of generating a tiny amount every time it was the capacity to make around 50 kilograms (100 pounds) within each chamber, which is at most significant.

The huge production of alkali became an important issue in addition, Nicolas Leblanc succeeded in developing an approach to produce salt carbonate as early as 1791. Sulfuric acid was incorporated with salt chloride through the process of Leblanc to create the salt sulfate as well as hydrochloric acid. For the production of salt carbonate and calcium sulfide, salt was created using limestone (calcium carbonate) as well as coal. The salt carbonate that was soluble was separated from calcium sulfide, by adding water. This led to the release of the production of numerous toxins (the hydrochloric acid was initial vented into the atmosphere while calcium sulfide remained the most ineffective of waste products). But, in contrast to soda ash that was produced by burning specific plant species (barilla) also known as kelp that were the primary sources of soda ash and it is potash (potassium carbonate) created from wood and ash, the artificial soda ash proved to be cheaper.

Both of these substances were vital in their own right because they paved the way to many of new developments. This includes however not only the substitution of many smaller businesses with cheaper and easily manageable processes. The fabric, glass soap and paper markets all utilized salt carbonate. Sulfuric acid was first employed for picking (eliminating the rust off of) steel and iron and for lightening fabric.

Cement

Joseph Aspdin, a British bricklayer and contractor, invented an industrial process to make portland cement around 1824. It was an important development for the building and construction sector. A mixture of limestone and clay is stirred until it reaches around 1,400 degree C (2,552 degrees F) before being ground into a fine powder and then mixed with sand, water, and gravel, to create concrete. A few years later, while construction began on the Thames Tunnel, the renowned English engineer Marc Isambard Brunel used Portland cement. In the following years cement was extensively used during the construction of the London sewer system.

Making Glass

The ancient Greece as well as Rome made glass. It was at the time beginning of the 1900s, the process of cylinder is a new method for creating glass, was invented in Europe. It was the Chance Bro used this innovation to produce sheet glass during the year 1832. They climbed up to the very high-end of the plate and window glass industry. The development made it possible for larger sheets made of glass created with no disturbances, freeing the interior space as well as the structure's the fenestration. Crystal Palace Crystal Palace is the peak of the use of glass sheets with a distinctive and unique form.

Devices for Making Paper

Nicholas Louis Robert, who was a member of the Saint-Leger Didot family of France invented a method that could create a permanent sheets of paper over the loop of wire in 1798. Following the loans of Sealy along with Henry Fourdrinier, who were stationers in London The device for making paper is referred to as the Fourdrinier. The Fourdrinier model regardless of all its modifications and improvements it is the preferred method for manufacturing paper in the present.

Mining

The coal mining industry began to develop in the UK particularly in South Wales, at an earlier period. The pits were usually small bell pits that were formed by an intersection of coal across the top of the area prior to steam engines were installed, and were abandoned as coal was extracted. Other times, if the geology permitted coal to be pulled out through an adit, or a mining drifts went down the hill's side. The use of shaft mining was attempted in a few areas, however it was difficult to eliminate water. could be a major blocking block. The process could be done through the transfer of pails of water through the shaft or an or a sough (a tunnel built into the hill in order to drain the mine). Whatever the case, the water must be taken away at a point at which it can flow via gravity down an aquifer or ditch.

Transport

Transport across the land was carried out by roads and rivers that were accessible prior to the time at the beginning of Industrial Revolution, with seaside vessels being used to transport large objects through the ocean. Canals were not widely constructed due to the fact that wagonways were employed to transport coal from rivers to facilitate shipping. In the land, animals supplied everything needed to power. At sea, ships provided power sources. Horse-drawn trains first came to market towards the close of the 18th century. They were then steam engines followed during the first decade of the 19th century. Between 1750-1830, improvements in cruising technologies increased average cruise speed by about 50%.

Through a turnpike road network, canal and waterway system, as well as a railway network and train network, the Industrial Revolution enhanced Britain's transport roads. The basic materials and items could be transported quicker and at lesser cost than they were before. Improved transport has also made it easier for the rapid spread of fresh concepts.

Navigation along various British streams was improved prior to and after the Industrial Revolution by removing obstacles by reversing the course of bends, expanding the width and length of channels and constructing locks to facilitate navigation. In 1750 Britain was home to more than 1,600 km (about 1,600 miles) of navigable rivers and streams.

The canals and rivers allowed the transport of massive materials into the countryside over miles with a minimal cost. This was due to the fact that horses could transport a barge carrying an enormous weight that was larger than what a cart can.

In the time during the Industrial Revolution, France was known for its great road system, but many of the roads in the European Continent and in the UK were not in good conditions and severely rutted.

All through during the Industrial Revolution, roadway transport efficiency increased while travel expenditures plummeted. The performance of long-distance transport almost doubled between 1690-1840, as stage-coaching output increased to 4 times.

The prevalence of cheap iron puddled following 1800, the invention of a rolling mill creating rails, and development of the high pressure steam engine, in fact all around 1800, helped make trains feasible.

Chapter 10: Social And Societal Results Of The Revolution

These innovations triggered an entirely new way of work, and a completely more different life style for many individuals. Technology was taking over. Processes were automated, and civilisations needed to adjust. This chapter will go through some of the changes that occurred in this section.

The Factory Approach

Before the Industrial Revolution, farming employed many workers, either in the form of self-employed farmers renting landowners, renters or landowners as well as landless farmers. Family members all over the globe made their own yarns and woven their own fabrics and even designed their own clothing. To produce for the market, houses weaved and spun yarn. India, China, and some parts of Iraq as well as in the Middle East produced many the global cotton textiles from the beginning of

Industrial Revolution, while Europeans created linen and wool items.

In the 16th century, the putting-out method, in where farmers and townpeople created products for markets within their own homes were in use throughout the UK as well. It was commonly called a home market. Weaving and spinning were common in the putting-out process. Typically, merchant capitalists provide the raw materials, and paid workers per piece and supervised the selling of their product. Employees' embezzlement of materials and substandard quality was routine difficulties. Also, the putting-out process had problems with logistics in taking and dispersing the basic supplies in addition to acquiring finished products.

The cottagers were able to pay for early weaving and spinning equipment for example, a 40 spindle jenny, which cost around 6 pounds during the year 1792.

Other equipment like spinning frames and spinning mules and power looms, all ended in being expensive (especially in the case of water-powered equipment) which led to the factory being owned by capitalists.

When we were at that time during the Industrial Revolution, most fabric market workers were married women with kids. This is a lot of orphans. They were employed for 12 to 14 days a week typically, taking only weekends free. When it was the time during the winter months where farm work was scarce and the weather was a bit chilly, it was common for women to be employed in factories. It was difficult to find or keep employees due to the lack of a suitable transportation system as well as long working hours and poor pay. In the absence of a need, numerous people, including farmers and laborers in the agricultural sector, with nothing to sell other than their labor were eventually commercial laborers.

(Threshing device, British Agricultural Revolution).

Karl Marx was critical of changes in relationship between factory workers and the cottagers and farmers however, he appreciated the increase in productivity that innovation brought.

The Typical Civilian's Requirement of Living

Certain financial specialists, such as Robert E. Lucas, Jr. consider that the real impact from the Industrial Revolution was that it improved the efficiency of people "For this, the first time in the history of mankind that the necessities for the vast majority of people are beginning to increase gradually ... The classical economics experts do not make any mention of this type of financial behavior, not even as a possible scenario." Some, on the other side, argue that even though it is true that the Industrial Revolution saw extraordinary development in terms of efficiency and general abilities, living standards for many people didn't increase substantially until the latter part of the 19th and early 20th centuries however, many ways, people's demands for food and shelter decreased in the first years of industrialization. For instance study studies have shown that the real earnings of Britain just increased by 15% from 1780 between 1850 and 1780, and the lives were cut short.

Also, during that time of Industrial Revolution, the typical size of people decreased it was evident that their nutritional well-being was also declining. The real wages weren't enough to cover increasing food costs.

The lifespan of children increased significantly in that time of the Industrial Revolution. Between 1730 and 1749, 74.5 percent of the children born in London died before they reached the age of five. as compared to 31.8 per cent in 1810-1829.

In the 1950s to the mid-1980s, financial and social historians debated whether the economic revolution was a positive or negative impact on life needs.

In the 1950s Henry Phelps Brown and Sheila V. Hopkins published an array of papers that established an academic consensus that the majority of people especially those on the lowest levels of society were suffering significant losses in their daily lives.

The country saw a dramatic increase in the wages of workers from 1813 until 1913.

Real Estate

The new industrial and production cities, as well as service centers such as Edinburgh and London witnessed a dramatic population increase in the 19th century.

Most important was the funding aspect and was managed by the building societies, which dealt straight with large contracting firms.

The most common type of lease was private leasing by real estate owners. As per P. Kemp, this is usually beneficial to people who rented. Since there was no funds to provide adequate housing for all, poor young people were pushed to reside in overcrowded, run-down areas. There was a high rate of death with a significant increase in infant mortality as well as tuberculosis in young children because of the absence of clean drinking water, sanitation and healthcare facilities in public. Typhoid and Cholera were both endemic because of contaminated drinking water. It was rare to see starvation in cities, similar to the ones that destroyed Ireland in 1840.

These conditions led to an abundance of writing that criticized the doors off. The Situation of the Working Class in England (1844) written by Friedrich Engels, one of the founders of the Socialist movement, outlined streets in Manchester as well as other mill towns, where the workers lived in shacks and rough shanties with some that were not completely restricted, and some having dirt flooring. There were small roads between the unevenly shaped lot and the houses that were within these shantytowns. Bathrooms were not readily and readily available. It was an extremely high density of people. However, not everyone lived in such dire circumstances. In the Industrial Revolution also brought to the world a new middle class of clerks, business people as well as supervisors and engineers, who enjoyed much higher living standards.

Public health legislation that regulates the health and sewage sectors as well as real estate construction and building made conditions better throughout the nineteenth century. Engels notes in his introduction in his edition of 1892 that the vast majority of problems he wrote about in 1844 had significantly improved. In 1875, the General Public Health Act of 1875 for example has led to hygiene-conscious byelaw for terraced homes.

Nutrition and Food

In the latter half of the nineteenth century, uncontrollable appetites and a poor diet was the norm for most of humanity which included Britain as well as France. The life span of France was approximately 35 years, and around 40 in Britain up to 1750 because of cravings. The people of the US at that time was well-nourished and much larger on average and had a lifespan duration of 45 to 50 years. However, living spans of the U.S.A. was reduced by a few years in the middle of the nineteenth century. In the time of what was called the Antebellum puzzle and the amount of food consumed per capita decreased as well.

The Corn Laws (from about 1815to 1846) have had a detrimental impact on the food supply within the U.K.. They were the Corn Laws, which put taxes on grain imported from abroad, were implemented in order to ensure that rates were high enough to ensure that local producers were able to profit. In the beginning during the Great Irish Starvation, the Corn Laws were reversed.

The initial Industrial Revolution innovations, like mechanized fabric, iron and coal, were able in the end, but they did lower the costs of food.

Before the Industrial Revolution, food supply rose throughout both the U.K. and the Netherlands because of improved agriculture practices. However according to Thomas Malthus mentioned, population also grew.

It is known as the Malthusian trap has been the term that was given to the situation which was later removed by transport improvement like canals and enhanced highways, and steamships. At the time in the Industrial Revolution, railways and steamships were built.

Industrialization and Literacy

The 18th century was when the markets of the present were developed with England and Scotland in which farmers, particularly in Scotland have astonished amounts of education. It was possible to collaborate with skilled artisans skilled workers, experienced managers, and supervisors who could supervise the newly developed coal mines and fabric mills. A lot of jobs were not experienced, and in factories for fabric, children from as young as eight years old helped in household chores, and also supplemented families' earnings. The kids were often taken from school for work in the factory alongside their parents and caretakers. In the late nineteenth century however, the common labor force were prevalent across Western Europe, and British markets had shifted upwards and required hiring numerous engineers and skilled workers that could be able to follow the technical instructions and deal with difficult problems. In order to be employed, one had to be educated.

Durable Goods and Clothes

The customers made money through reduced prices on clothing and household products such as cast iron cooking equipment as well as ranges for cooking and space heating during the next decade. The majority of individuals living from Europe were able to control tea, coffee, cigarettes, sugar and even chocolate. Between the 1660s and about 1750, the consumer revolution in England witnessed a significant increase in consumption and the variety of luxury items and goods used by individuals from every walk of life. Selling and buying options became much more efficient and effective, as the use of transport and business innovations grew. Because of the expanding textile market in the northern part of England and the suit in three pieces was made more accessible to people.

Wedgwood's porcelain and fine china tableware, founded through Josiah Wedgwood in the year 1759, was beginning to become the norm at dining tables. Through the 18th century, the rise of success and social movements led to a rise in the number of people who earned a salary that was not reusable to use, and the commercialization of goods for individuals and not just items for families was beginning to be seen in the same way, along with the rising position of the products as status symbolisms that were linked to the evolution of fashions and desire for visual attraction (of of which Wedgwood was one of the leaders).

Companies in new companies across a variety of market segments popped up across the cities and regions all over the U.K.. Chocolate was among the industries that expanded rapidly. Polly Russell, a food historian, says she believes that "Thanks to the Industrial Revolution and the customers that it brought, chocolates and biscuits became market-leading products. They were budget-friendly delight by mid-nineteenth century and the business was increasing. Huntley & Palmers in Reading, Carr's of Carlisle, and McVitie's in Edinburgh changed from a small, family-owned company to modern production processes ".

Chocolate bars were first invented in 1847 by Fry's from Bristol. In the year 1868, when Cadbury of Birmingham introduced a heart-shaped package of chocolates to celebrate Valentine's Day in the year 1868, they became the first to advertise the link between love and confectionery.

Growing literacy rates, industrialization, as well as the construction and building of the railroad created a market for affordable, well-known and popular literature to the general public, as well as the ability to distribute the literature widely. In order to meet this demand the cent was introduced during the 1830s.

The Guardian called cent dreadfuls "the Victorian equivalent of computer games" as well as "Britain's first exposure to mass-produced pop culture aimed at the youngsters." Over one million children had their books sold every week during the 1860s and the 1870s. The Paris Review called Charles Dickens an "authorpreneur" due to his misuse of new technologies to market his work, such as innovative printing presses, higher sales from marketing and railway expansion. The novel that he published first,

Pickwick Documents (1836) Pickwick Documents (1836), turned out to be a publishing adventure, producing a myriad of follow-ups and gadgets including Pickwick togies, cards, porcelain figurines and Weller boot polish, Weller puzzles Weller Boot Polish, and even joke books. "Literature" isn't an expansive enough classification that would be appropriate for Pickwick as outlined by Nicholas Dames in The Atlantic. The genre has its own definition that we refer to in the context of "home entertainment."

Urbanization

In the 18th century, the advent of market-based capitalism has resulted in significant urbanisation as well as the development of great cities starting in Europe and later in different countries, as the new opportunities brought a large number of residents from the backwoods into cities. The percentage of city dwellers at the time of 1800, as compared to approximately 50 percent in the present (the dawn at the beginning of 21st Century). Manchester was home to 10000 people by 1717. However, it grew to 2.3 million in 1911.

Women and Families Affected

The impact on women's status of Industrial Revolution and commercialism in general, on women's position is a topic that has been criticized by historians of women's history.

The downside is that Alice Clark really believed that the advent of industrialization at the end of 17th century England affected women's status because they were stripped of their importance financially. Women played a role in numerous aspects of market-based and agriculture in 16th century England as per Clark. Women were a key part in the administration of farms and various trades as well as estates that were landed, since home production was the primary method for production. The financial responsibilities of women allowed them to enjoy a degree of equal status with their spouses. However, when industrialization grew during the 17th century Clark states there was a heightened divide of labor with one spouse working in paid in the outside world while the other partner was tasked with house chores which were awaited. Women of lower class were forced into low-paying work in the middle and upper classes, while middle- and upper-class women had to live the confines of their homes, working as a the household. Thus, commercialism was negative effects on famous women.

Ivy Pinchbeck, in a more optimistic analysis, suggests that industrialization was the catalyst to women's rights.

Tilly Scott and Scott have highlighted the significance to women's role in English historical times, while recognizing three periods. Women provided a large portion of the family's needs in the preindustrial period, where output was mostly used to support home use. Second stage of industrialisation was known as the "family wage economy" that is, where the entire family, which includes spouse, partner in marriage as well as the older children, were dependent on the incomes shared by all of their family members. The "family consumer economy" in which the household is the main source of income and females are employed with great numbers in the areas of retail and clerical to help meet increasing demands for usage this is the 3rd and contemporary stage.

While Europe was swept away with The Industrial Revolution, middle-class families were defined by the notion of thrift and a consistent efforts. The class of people who were less fortunate was "voluntary and self-imposed- caused by idleness as well as thriftiness, apathy and misbehavior" as per Samuel Smiles' book Self-Help.

Working Conditions

The Industrial Revolution saw a middle group of industrialists and business people win against the gentlemen and nobles in terms of social structures. The common worker had more possibilities in the modern factories and mills, however they often had to be subjected to harsh working conditions that included long work hours controlled by equipment. As late as 1900 the majority of commercial employees in the US were employed for a full day of 10 hours (about 12 hours for the market for steel) earning between up to 20%-40% less than what was thought to be necessary for a comfortable life. However, the majority of employees in the textile market and the textile market, without doubt the largest by terms of employment included children and women.

The industrial world "was the equivalent of a desert which the workers had to make accessible by themselves" for employees in the working classes. In addition, the harsh working conditions were in place prior to that Industrial Revolution. Before the Industrial Revolution, life was extremely rigid and often difficult. Kid work, filthy living conditions as well as long hours of work were the norm.

The industrial revolution was the result of industrialization. The commercial model helped the growth of cities through large numbers of people into cities to pursue the dream factories. Mills and market of Manchester were referred to as "Cottonopolis" and dubbed the first city in the world to be commercialized is a prime example of this. Between 1771 and 1831 Manchester witnessed a sixfold increase in the population. Between 1811 and 1851 Bradford was able to grow by 50 percent every 10 years. By 1851, less than 50% of the inhabitants were born in the city.

Furthermore Between 1815 and 1939 20 percent of Europe's inhabitants emigrated due to the effects of poverty as well as growth in population development as well as the loss of craftsmen and peasant farmers production. These people were enticed due to the huge demand for work, the easy availability of land, as well as transportation costs that were low. Yet, many were unhappy at their new homes which led to seven million people to go back to Europe. This massive movement had huge economic effects. In 1890, overseas Europeans as well as their descendants comprised just 1% of the population in the world; in 1930, they accounted for 11percent. The Americas were the main beneficiaries of this massive diaspora with the majority of it concentrated within America. United States.

For the majority of the 19th century, manufacturing was carried out in mills of a smaller size most of which were powered by water and built in order to satisfy regional demands. Every mill would eventually have its own steam engine, as well as chimney, which would provide an effective circulation of steam through the boiler.

In a few markets, the move towards factory production was not as controversial. Factory owners attempted to improve working and real property conditions for their employees members. Robert Owen, well known for his early efforts in making working conditions better at New Lanark mills, was one of the pioneers. New Lanark mills and often considered to be one of the earliest social movement's most fundamental theorists was not the only one among the pioneers of reform.

Warmley close to Bristol near Bristol, was an integral brass mill as early as 1746. The basic material was gathered, then merged with brass and then was transformed into pans, pins wire, pans, and other goods. The site was also home to a housing facility for workers. Some of the early manufacturers who employed the factory model comprised Josiah Wedgwood and Matthew Boulton (whose Soho Manufactory was completed around 1766.).

Child Labor

While during the Industrial Revolution led to a increase in population, the odds of remaining young didn't improve despite significant decreases in baby mortality rates.

There was no guarantee of educational opportunities, and the kids were expected to work. Employers could offer a child more than a grown-up, regardless of the fact they performed the same and there was no need for strength or endurance to run an industrial device. Moreover, there were not any educated adults working in the workplace simply because the business system was completely new. At the beginning of the Industrial Revolution, between the 18th and 19th centuries that made child labor the preferred method of production. The year 1788 saw nearly two-thirds of workers working during the year of 143, which was the cotton mills powered by water in England in England and Scotland were kids.

The concept of kid labor was present prior up to Industrial Revolution, but it became more apparent with the increase in population and education rates grew. The majority of children were forced to be in gruelling conditions with a lower pay rate than the older generation, earning about ten to 20% of an average man's wage.

The reports describing the crimes, particularly within coal mines and textile factories, were published in order to highlight the plight of youngsters. A general protest in the public particularly among those in the upper and middle class, contributed to changes in the lives of workers in the midst of their careers.

Politicians and the federal government fought to stop child labor with legislation however, factory owners would not agree to do so. Some believed that by offering their children cash in order to buy food items to avoid starvation, they were aiding the dependent and clingy, while some simply allowed the low-cost labor. It was the Factory Acts, passed in 1833 and 1844, in Britain they were the very first guidelines for universally regulating children's labor. Kids who were younger than nine could not be employed or work at night. Children were also not permitted to work after dark as well as the working hours of children under 18 was restricted to twelve hours. Factory inspectors oversee their compliance with the law, but their absence made it difficult to enforce. (needs citation) Children and women weren't allowed working in mines until 10 years after. In spite of the fact that regulations like these reduced the quantity of child workers in the mines, child labor was prevalent across Europe and in the USA up to the turn of the century.

Slavery's Growth and Cotton

The low-cost cotton fabric increased the demand for cotton raw, which were typically utilized in subtropical zones that it was grown in and there was not much pure cotton being accessible for export. This meant that the cost of raw cotton were increased. From two million pounds in in 1700, to five million pounds by 1781, and up to 56 million pounds by the period of 1800.

British manufacturing increased dramatically. The turning point is American Eli Whitney's invention of the cotton gin during 1792. It was a green-seeded crop that became profitable due to that which allowed massive plantations of servants to expand across the United States, Brazil, as well as the West Indies. Production of cotton in USA was at its peak of 35 million pounds during 1800. It was 50% of the production exporting. Plantations of cotton in America proved to be extremely efficient and profitable, and were able to satisfy demands. The "cotton shortage" that was triggered by Civil War in the USA led to increased production in other areas of the world particularly European inhabitants living in Africa.

Contamination of the Environment

In the course of throughout the Industrial Revolution, rising levels of smoke pollution in the atmosphere prompted the beginning of the eco-conscious movement. Following

1900, the large quantity of chemical discharges from commercial industries caused the increase of abandoned human waste as a result from the development of large factories. In addition, due to the massive synchronized development in the coal intake. commercial cities experienced unbeatable amounts of pollution from the air.

The Alkali Acts, passed in 1863 within the U.K., were the first major, modern eco-friendly guidelines to control the dangerous air pollution (gaseous hydrochloric acid) produced by the Leblanc process. It is utilized to produce soda Ash. To combat the pollution there was an inspector for Alkali and four sub-inspectors were appointed. Inspectorate's responsibilities grew with time until they culminated with the Alkali Order of 1958, which governed all major big companies that produced dust, smoke or even the odor of fumes.

From 1812between 1812 and 1820, a gas market exploded throughout British cities. This method led to extremely harmful sewage flowing to waterways and drains. Gas service suppliers have been slapped with by the law numerous times, in a variety of problematic actions. They frequently lost, and then changed their bad practices. The 1820s saw London was awash with scandal. City of London charged gas firms with polluting the Thames as well as poisoning fish.

In order to control toxicity, the Parliament created corporations charters. In 1850, the first market began to emerge to the United States, leading to lawsuits and contamination.

Regional experts and reformers were the first to acknowledge the environmental destruction and pollution in the commercial city, specifically from 1890 onwards, and then launching grassroots efforts to demand to implement reforms.

The contamination of air and water are the most frequent topics of concerns. It is believed that the Coal Smoke Reduction Society was formed in of 1898, in U.K., making it one of the longest-running eco-friendly non-government companies around the globe. It was created by the artist Sir William Blake Richmond, who was depressed by the gloom of coal smoke.

Despite previous laws in the past, the public Health Act of 1875 mandated that fireplaces and heaters make use of their own fumes. The act also imposed fees on factories that produced large quantities of smoke that was black. It was also the Smoke Reduction Act of 1926 extended the scope of law's provisions to encompass other types of emissions, such as soot, ash and gritty particles. It is additionally, it gave city officials the authority to establish their own regulations.

Chapter 11: Transport

Ability to move individuals and goods from one location to the next became a key element in optimizing manufacturing during the industrial revolution. In the time that it was the American Industrial Revolution started around in the early 1800s factories were built near raw material. In the event that factories required to be located further away from their sources the industrialists favored locating the factories near transportation facilities that was possible via the waters. It was due to the hard work of men such as Cornelius Vanderbilt, a man who was a tireless worker to create a stable transportation system across American rivers.

Cornelius Vanderbilt

Cornelius Vanderbilt was born in Port Richmond in New York to the family of farmers and boatmen. An avid sea-farer since his earliest times, Vanderbilt dropped out of school in order to help on the boat of his father at age 11 years old. When he was sixteen He was skilled enough to have his own vessel. The boat was purchased by borrowing money from his father. Then he joined the New York-Staten Islands travel route.

Vanderbilt was an excellent captain, however his skills were even superior to managing the business aspect of his vessel. In his time that the War of 1812 was breaking out, the captain of 18 years old had only a few vessels. He was awarded a contract to supply municipal outposts in the city and utilized the funds to increase his fleet more. One of the vessels Vanderbilt purchased was his brother's Schooner. He with his father on buying and selling groceries. But in 1818 impressed by the scale and the profits from steamships Vanderbilt agreed to oversee New York tycoon Thomas Gibbons steamships, and resigned his job as Captain of his own vessel.

Inclusion into the maritime travel and tourism industry

The very first job Vanderbilt had outside his family's fleet was an extremely competitive field. He was a mentor for a large enterprise, Gibbons taught Vanderbilt that it was all about determination and perseverance against opposition. Gibbons was chosen because the man of his age had proven to be a steadfast captain, even on small rowboats. The boat owners who were his colleagues gave him the title "Commodore" which he accepted the title.

At the time, New York was an extremely growing city of approximately two hundred thousand residents and around one hundred thousand additional residents from nearby cities that was New Jersey. Transporting both goods and people between these two cities was extremely important. The control over the shipping routes brought enormous business satisfaction and prosperity as well. Thomas

Gibbons was embroidered in an affidavit with Aaron Ogden and his steamship firm. They had monopoly rights over New York waters, partly due to his association with the inventor of steamboats Robert Fulton. Aged Gibbons could not face Ogden's fierceness. Ogden and was never afraid to use his contacts in city halls for an advantage. He offered Vanderbilt the freedom to do whatever it was he had to accomplish to force Ogden out of his business. Vanderbilt proved a perfect candidate for the job making use of price cutting as well as legal action to grow market shares.

Beginning in 1818 Gibbons and Ogden filed a lawsuit to resolve their disagreement, which became an issue of state as well as federal discussion. Ogden was seeking to keep the permit granted to the State of New York to be the only steamer on the New Jersey-New York line and Gibbons required proof there was no evidence that states like

New York could not dictate the maritime industry in relation to commerce with states other than its own. Legal suits bind Ogden by court dates and caused him to lose his job, whereas Vanderbilt was unaffected by the entire process. He was an individual who flourished in the face of pressure. Despite the fact that Gibbons was unsuccessful in the lawsuit at the time of his death in 1820. He maintained the operation of the steamship until 1824, when it was the time that Supreme Court ruled in his in his favor. Vanderbilt was a key player in the debacle by hiring the lawyer who later was successful in winning the case, and made a move against state-funded businesses Monopolies.

Being a captain of steamships in the exciting and bustling waterways that flowed through New York City, Vanderbilt could see an imminent expansion in the market. As farms increased their production as well as the growing population of urban areas the need for transportation of food items was rising rapidly. Furthermore, factories that were just established like textile manufacturing facilities had to move ingredients to production premises and then transport the final products onto the market. Being in control of the transportation routes ensured that the company could reap the benefits of the expanding American business without spending excessive amounts of money to set up factories.

However, as an entrepreneur by birth and an individual with distinct ideas of how business should be conducted, Vanderbilt would not stay with Gibbons the company for very many years. He was required to understand how to run a business and did so over the course of nine years when in charge of one of his steamboats. The time was time to launch his unique style of business and take on the world of steamship transportation.

Vanderbilt was involved in steamboats

While he ran Gibbons steamship Vanderbilt kept his private commercial interests. In the early 1820s, Vanderbilt was one of the main players of the New York sea transport, in part because he was the captain of one of the biggest steamers as well as a handful of smaller vessels. He would however not be able to manage the steamship for a long time. In 1826, the boss Thomas Gibbons passed away. The steamship business was passed onto William, his son William Gibbons, who showed little involvement in the family-owned business.

A few years later, Vanderbilt moved back to the captain of his steamers. The plan was to grow his fleet, and eventually acquire his share of the New York waters, which began with persuading William to buy the lines that he had created along with the steamer which operated these lines. Of course, William would be happy to do so, and sold the business for a profit to Vanderbilt by 1829. As the sole owner of managing the steamship Vanderbilt was eager to launch his own brand of rivalry against others.

His initial target is that of the Hudson River Steamboat Association (HRSA) cartel. The HRSA was created in 1832, to unite an association of steamboat owners along the Hudson River. The non-compete agreement and the profit-sharing arrangement granted the cartel a absolute control over all Hudson River ocean routes. Profits were then divided equally among owners and the participants would be guaranteed better margins than the exorbitant rates that the HRSA permitted them to cost. The idea for the cartel came from the mind by John Stevens, a man who was the son of an immediate beneficiary of the protected monopoly of state protection which Vanderbilt broke into two in 1824. This was the only difference, and it was because of in this manner, the monopoly was legal.

At the same time, Vanderbilt was increasing his market share and was gaining advantage over the competition, by slowly taking them out of the market and adding steamers to their existing lines. The strategy was first implemented in 1830, when he cut rates on steamers in huge margins as high than half. Competitors were unable meet the lowest prices and were compelled to take one at a time to shut down their vessels. In only one year Vanderbilt was able to take over his Long Island Sound estuary from his rivals.

To show his final kindness, he offered to purchase the steamers in a state of disarray with the help of intermediaries, in order in order to not annoy the owners in distress. Although the owners weren't willing to sell but they were obliged to make the sale when their vessels sat rotting on the shore, with no passengers on board, simply because Vanderbilt was able to take the entire fleet. The choice was between bankruptcy and the possibility of recovery and Vanderbilt did not hesitate to make use of this to force them to bow according to his demands.

This was to become a primary plan of attack when The Commodore was toe-to-toe against rivals in the near future. One of the rare occasions where he didn't need to use bullying tactics was when he purchased the brother's Peekskill, New York line. This gave him an advantage on the operational side of his position on the Hudson River. The only time the strategy totally fell short was when he had interactions with a steamboat owner called Daniel Drew.

Drew was among the crew members of the Hudson through Vanderbilt's reign as price terror. In contrast to other ships, Drew was able to repel Vanderbilt's assault and even cause him to suffer as well. It was due in part to the fact that Drew was a devoted client and also because he cut the prices of his services to close to Vanderbilt's. The issue was further complicated because Drew was an active part of the HRSA as well as a participant in the tensions between the HRSA as well as Vanderbilt. The cartel as well as Vanderbilt were making their intention to rule the steamboat business within New York clear. In 1833, both the cartel as well as Vanderbilt were able to avoid a confrontation between themselves, however tensions were not low. Then, in the end they both were in agreement that the war on prices could continue to harm the respective companies for a long time. A secret agreement to end the price war was formed.

In 1834, a war of words was fought among Vanderbilt as well as the cartel. They were both eyeing the other's territories: the North River of the Hudson for Vanderbilt and Hastings on Hudson to the cartel. Vanderbilt utilized a sophisticated lease and ownership operations in the cartel that involved his steamer Westchester. Drew and Vanderbilt's alliance proved beneficial, allowing each of them to benefit from

Drew's position by getting Drew to lease and manage the Westchester across the New York to Albany line. At first, Drew conformed to the cartel's rates. However, because the Westchester was a larger vessel that was larger than the Vanderbilt, Drew and Vanderbilt did not earn enough money to cover the costs that the vessel allowed, while they shared profits in a smaller vessel.

Beginning in 1834 both of them cut the price for Westchester by half, bringing it down to just one dollar. The two also added two brand new vessels - they named the Champion and Nimrod as part of their fleet. The two ships were named "The People's Line" and took advantage of the the patriotic spirit of the president Andrew Jackson to attract passengers. When the war on prices grew, Vanderbilt dropped prices to the 50 cent mark, and later down to nothing by the close in the calendar year. Due to their ships being large, the expense to operate them was paid back through a charge higher for entertainment and food.

In the final quarter of the year, HRSA was facing serious financial difficulties. Their vessels had made significant losses and their future looked at risk. The broker was charged with making a deal with Vanderbilt to stop the price war. They succeeded in reaching a settlement which paid him handsomely to stay out of getting on the Hudson River for the next 10 years. The first payment was a generous 100,000 in 1835, and a further $5,000 over the following 9 years Vanderbilt got a fair amount for running his steamboat business and elsewhere. He returned to Long Island Sound.

The 1830s saw the first time that textile mills located in the New England region were increasing in importance and size. They were now supplying the entire of America with cotton which was competing with imported material from Britain. The cotton had to be shipped across into the Deep South over the Long Island Sound waterways to make it to factories. The operation in the region made a lot of money. Vanderbilt began a purchase of the steamboats remaining that operated in the waters of this region, and became the only one to link the railroads in Boston to the transporting cotton ports in New York. Over the next several years, Vanderbilt was hawkish in protecting his land. Newcomers into Long Island Sound Long Island Sound were driven by the same methods which had proved so effective to defeat the HRSA.

Exiting into the ocean

As any businessman who was ambitious, Vanderbilt was soon hunting for new areas to take on. The steamboat industry was one of his main interests. Vanderbilt saw and tried to capitalize on the opportunity of the California gold rush in 1949. Many thousands relocated across the continent in search of gold mines that were located in

Sierra Nevada, Coloma, San Francisco, Shasta, and Northern California. You could not move that long distances from one area of America to the next, and the 3000 miles that separated these two places became an enormous barrier to prospective buyers and huge obstacles to the transfer of gold to the cash-rich market of in the East Coast. The quick action of investors such as Vanderbilt assisted in facilitating prospectors' movement at high personal profit.

He persuaded a handful of steamboat owners to establish an Accessory Transit Company which moved people from across the East Coast right into the goldfields. The journey was multi-tiered and began with New York, connected to ports San Juan del Norte or Mosquito Coast in the American Isthmus. The route then crossed into the rivers that flowed through Rio San Juan and Lake Nicaragua and finally to the city of Rivas. Stagecoaches could even be arranged for all the way up to San Francisco. It was a great option for prospectors and many of them flocked to the Accessory Transit Company in their thousands of dollars, and even $300 for an efficient and easy travel.

One of the partners who invested of ATC ATC was a successful businessman and ex-politician Joseph White. In recognition of the potential for the gold rush White tried to get Vanderbilt out of the business. Vanderbilt was willing to let his shares go, but increased the cost of the vessels in 1852. The following year, when Vanderbilt was taking an extended family vacation in Europe, White conspired with his third-party partner to stop him from receiving the cash due to him by the proceeds of selling the ships. They were both forced to settle the debt they owed to him after Vanderbilt went back home to America and set up a competing business to help prospectors move across Europe. After just a few months of price cut-offs and price increases, he convinced them to settle every penny of the money owed to him.

Over the course of the next several decades, Vanderbilt brought his old reputation of brutal price battles to Atlantic oceans. He fought shipping titans such as Edward Collins the Collins Line is the largest line of the Atlantic Ocean, and drove the Collins Line out of their business. It was an impressive accomplishment due to the fact that Collins Line was Collins Line was heavily subsidized by the federal government of America in order to compete with that of the British Cunard Line.

To gain an advantage against other steamers along the same route, Vanderbilt had purchased the Allaire Iron Works, the firm that produced steamship engines. In this means he could earn profit despite competitors who tried to force them out of his business. The the conditions in Nicaragua changed to confer him with a bigger advantage on the New York-San Francisco highway.

In 1854 In 1854, it was reported that the American Navy had started bombarding the facility ATC that were used for embarking as well as getting passengers off from San Juan at the request by local town officials. In the following year was when a prospecting filibuster, named William Walker, who had received the support of Joseph White, took over the administration of Nicaragua and undermining White by taking over the ATC infrastructure there.

The development could be considered a blessing disguise since Vanderbilt only recently began purchasing ownership back of the ATC. There was a conflict with the present owners, who tried to prevent Vanderbilt from acquiring ownership of the vessels through White's power as the president of Nicaragua. The American government was unable to intervene due to the fact that the region was at war and the international policy at the time was strongly against interference. The fact that this region was plagued by conflict and wars, was a huge help to Vanderbilt to get control back by an amiable government which could allow Vanderbilt to return the ships he had seized.

However, after obtaining his assets returned Vanderbilt was denied access to the waters that flow through Nicaragua. He decided to seek an alternative to taking advantage of the gold rush and not involve his political stance in the local area. He's entry on the Nicaragua route upset two major steamship firms that were The Pacific Mail Steamship Company and the US Mail Steamship Company, which led him to reach a settlement that paid him monthly $40,000. The amount increased to $56,000 by 1858.

Vanderbilt was able to come up with an idea to link his Caribbean Sea and the Atlantic Ocean to the Pacific Ocean in the mid-1850s. He was granted the permission to build the Nicaragua Canal with the sole supervision of steamer traffic in the area, which was valid until 1861. The political turmoil of Nicaragua and the eruptions of the Momotombo volcano rendered the idea impossible to realize.

It was difficult to get involved in the transcontinental transportation business without being involved in the national political scene. Conflicts with Nicaragua was a clear example of this. However, even on the other side of America, Vanderbilt (and other famous businessmen who had businesses across the nation) were soon forced to choose a side after they were forced to choose between the Northern as well as Southern states fought during the American Civil War. Since he was an Northerner He backed those who fought in the Union Army. Although his age made him too old to fight, he still could give back by donating assets which by the time he was significant.

He was willing to transfer the Vanderbilt the largest steamer of his into the Navy. However, the maintenance and operational expense made it unaffordable for them to manage the vessel. Then, a few months later Merrimack, the Confederate ship Merrimack began to harass the Union group at Chesapeake Bay. The Union ships were unable to stand against the ironclad cruiser however, the Vanderbilt would not be hesitant to contribute to the military effort. The time was not much time for Vanderbilt to put the Merrimack out of service.

However, Vanderbilt's fascination with ships was waning. When the civil war was over the entrepreneur began selling his boats and shares in shipping firms. He was keen to move his foot on dry land where the increasing population of urban dwellers drove up demands for transport overland. Railroad lines for instance.

Vanderbilt was a railroad executive.

Vanderbilt began investing in railroads in the 1840s. He did this when the steamships were operating through the waterways that comprised Long Island Sound. Railroads linked ports for entry to the farms of the South as well as extending the routes through the factories that were located to New England. Railroads, which were unlimited by waterways were seen by Vanderbilt as great investment options.

The most successful company which used his shipping services across Long Island Sound Long Island Sound was The New York, Providence, and Boston Railroad. To get them to sell his services at a lower cost, he lowered rates for lines that competed and drove the price of stock to a low. He finally held enough shares in the firm to be able to buy it. He had to surrender control to purchase steamers for the ocean two years later, however Vanderbilt was an avid believer in the power of railroads in transforming transportation on land. While his main focus was in other areas, Vanderbilt served on the railway boards for a variety of railroads through the 1850s. These included Erie, New York and Harlem, Central New Jersey and Hartford as well as New Haven.

The 1860s was Vanderbilt's most important decade, as far as railroad transport is related. Vanderbilt began by taking over the management over the New York and Harlem railway firm by monopolizing the market for shares and claiming the presidentship of the business. Although the Harlem line was able to reach the middle of New York and was one of the railway lines which ran all the way into Manhattan but it was thought by many as useless and unimportant.

In the early 1860s, the largest railroad companies of New York each owned and operated their railways as Monopolies. Connectivity between competing railroads were not common, limiting the growth of New York in an enormous way. With the

Commodore however, it was not a problem. Once he purchased Harlem as his Harlem line, he aimed to extend it to additional routes. Only way he was able to achieve this was to purchase the businesses that controlled the routes he wanted for expansion.

A mistake he committed during his time at the time was to try and take control in Erie Railways, a company which operated from New York and Lake Erie. It was managed by Daniel Drew, Vanderbilt's old adversary. Although Vanderbilt was able to take control of the company away from current owners, he accidentally began a bitter battle with the financiers James Fisk and Jay Gould. Fisk and Gould were victorious through watering the shares of Erie Railroad, an antic which cost Vanderbilt nearly $7 million. The move also caused stock issuance structures as well as regulations that be put in place to stop this practices.

Vanderbilt was not deterred from buying railroads and, by 1870, he had enough railroad miles to build one of the biggest companies in America. With the ability to access routes in New York, Harlem, Michigan and New Jersey, he was capable of elevating the Harlem (his main railway corporation) into one of the largest companies across the nation. In order to manage the traffic of the various routes and to manage the traffic from all of them, he built his own Grand Central Depot on 42nd Street Manhattan. The tracks at the time were laid down via a cut. It was not until forty years after that the terminal was rebuilt with a tunnel and was renamed the Grand Central Terminal'

Vanderbilt was the most renowned transportation mogul in the Industrial revolution. Today, railroads and ocean steamers are far more than any other method for transport in the massive transport of passengers and goods. in 1869

Vanderbilt took a break from managing his business right following the death of his wife. He relocated to Ontario and was married by another woman by the name of Frank Armstrong Crawford. In the years that followed, he committed his entire life to charitable causes. The generosity of his was specifically directed towards the church. He donated $50,000 dollars to his wife's church. But the most significant contribution was made to the creation of Vanderbilt University in Nashville, TN. It was at that time the most significant charitable donation that was $1 million.

Carnegie Carnegie had his start within the industry of railroads in 1853 when he was operator of the telegraph working for the Pennsylvania Railroad Company. The exceptional and dedicated young man wowed his supervisors and was quickly elevated and eventually became director of the railroad's Western Division only six years after his start working in the telegraphing department. At the age of 18, Carnegie has paved his way into the world of business by working in the telegrapher's bureau and his career was never ever the same. Indeed, the road that he took while directing his department of the Western Division of the Pennsylvania Railroad Company was to bring him straight up to the top.

In his position as the director, he was directly working under the entrepreneur Thomas A. Scott and the president of the Pennsylvania Railroad Company John Edgar Thomson. Both Scott as well as Thomson were awestruck by Carnegie's dedication. Scott welcomed the young man in his wing and Thomson granted him the freedom to manage his department at a minimum of interruption. In his own way, Carnegie was an eager and swift student. His Western Division had thrived under his direction, enthralling not only Scott as well as Thomson as well as other top executives as well. One of the first lessons Carnegie took from Thomas Scott was on the positives of investing.

The 1860s were a time when railways constituted the most lucrative and largest sector in America. Railroad operators had all the cards in as when it came to transportation and in a country which was undergoing massive reforms to its industrial structure and a growing increasing demand for transport was ever increasing. Working as an executive at the railroad industry meant one was able to take advantage of underhanded deal deals known as quid pro quo such as insider trading, payments from agents of companies and trade groups seeking preferential treatment.

Carnegie was a shrewd investor that even with a pay in the range of $1,500 to $2,500 per one-year ($42,000 in 2018, adjusted for inflation) He was able to save a couple of dollars each month for investing. This means that early investment decisions

Carnegie did, with the direction under the direction of Thomas Scott no less, weren't legal. Indeed, Thomas Scott employed him as a third-party intermediary in a number transactions, including giving him the right to keep shares he acquired via insider trading.

In 1850, Carnegie was considerably rich. He held shares in exuberant companies like Adams Express - a courier services firm - and Theodore Tuttle's sleeping car business that offered the provision of room and board on long-distance trains. In the sleeping cars section, Carnegie was a man with a variety of loyalties. In addition to his fling with Theodore Woodruff, Carnegie also maintained a strong relationship and George Pullman, Woodruff's competitor. When Woodruff held the patents to the folding bed which allowed guests sleeping in the night with enough space, Pullman had the engineering and production capability to bring the idea.

Carnegie was in the right frame of mind to realize that should the two companies keep operating their businesses, they could end up suing one to stop the launching of sleeping railway car service. The services helped make rail travel much more pleasant over long distances. Since it was a travel service for long distances firm and it was the Pennsylvania Railroad Company (PRC) could have missed an opportunity in the event that Pullman and Woodruff were to compete. To prevent this from happening, Carnegie brokered a merger between the two firms. This merger was extremely beneficial for all three individuals in the mix.

Role in the Civil War

The merger of Pullman and Woodruff would be Carnegie's last act as head of the PRC prior to the time that his departure when Civil War broke out. At the age of 26, Carnegie was eligible for the draft, which was compulsory. But, Carnegie did not feel that his skills were in carrying arms. He believed that he could provide the most worthwhile contribution in the war effort being employed in the industrial complex in order to provide troops on the frontlines. The company paid him a replacement sum of $850 in order to pay the call in lieu of. But, he was content to go to Washington as the Superintendent of the Military Railways in 1861 at the request of his boss and mentor Thomas Scott. He was given the post of Vice Secretary of war by Lincoln and was given the command of logistical matters.

One of the first actions that Carnegie did after he arrived to Washington was enlisting the help of a railroad engineer John Wright in the establishment of the Freedom Iron Company. Carnegie was of the belief that conflict would be won by those who had the most advanced infrastructure. He didn't hesitate to make his Union Army up to par. Carnegie was the one responsible for railroads for troop movements in the lead up to and following during the First Battle of Bull Run. The final outcome from Bull Run Battle of Bull Run was an unforgiving routing of Union troops. In addition to the fact that it was a disaster for the soldier, he was suffering from sunstroke in the course of battle. Yet, he mustered the strength to oversee the transport of all the soldiers of Union army, including specially designed vehicles for wounded. After all troops had returned to base, did he decide the need to leave on absence in order to heal from his injury.

Scott was relieved by Scott Carnegie of his responsibilities for a couple of months, before he was sent back to the PRC Headquarters in Pittsburg. The cooler weather of Pittsburg will help him recuperate quicker from the sunstroke which he was suffering earlier. Relocating back to his previous post in Pittsburg was an extremely potent attraction for Carnegie. After stepping back from the battlefront

Carnegie rediscovered the importance of railroads as essential to victory. He began making plans for a better method of transporting soldiers via railroad.

One thing he noticed was that the economy was in a similar way that it did prior to the war. There was still plenty of opportunities for investment. Indeed, even with the bulk of the of the business industry being distracted by conflict, the stock market and the acquisitions sector was extremely lucrative. While he worked on the master plan of the most efficient method of sending soldiers to rails in the war, he also took time to work on his personal goals in investing.

In 1862, for instance He joined engineering brothers John and Shiffler in 1862 to establish The Piper and Shiffler Company. This company's goal was making iron bridges that would enable Union forces to traverse the rivers using their massive armaments. Although the project was a public service however, the entrepreneur still earned an impressive profit at the conclusion in the calendar year. That gave him the foundation for becoming an entrepreneurial social entrepreneur transformed into in the conflict. He was able to come up with ways to allow private firms to take on the huge projects the government had no resources to complete and yet attract the financier.

A logistics (railroad and Telegraph) method he set out to plan back in the aftermath of the loss in Bull Run proved to be enough when Union and Confederate troops met at Gettysburg. The Union victory in Gettysburg is largely because of the successful utilization of railroads for moving troops. This was something Carnegie was tasked with right from the beginning. When the war broke out in 1865 it was the time that there was a sense that the Civil War was over, and the Union won. Carnegie was on vacation in Europe to celebrate, however it was actually an official holiday during which he was granted an significant patent on wrought iron.

Post-war activities

In the course of war, Carnegie's view that railroads were an significant means of transport was affirmed. The Battle at Bull Run had been lost due to the fact that the Confederacy made use of their railroads in a better way than Carnegie did railroads within the Union territory. The Confederacy decided to focus its attention on the purposeful laying of railroad tracks and focusing on current war requirements and the potential future reuse. While managing the building of the railway tracks that he realized iron is actually the main component of railway.

Keystone Bridge Company

At the end of 1865 Carnegie received a job as the newly appointed Chief of Staff for the Pennsylvania Railroad Company. He declined the invitation, preferring to devote all of his time to the investments that he made in the past. There were also new investments outside of railroads and iron, which he planned to explore - bridges.

Railroads had to have bridges that crossed river valleys that were deep however, the wooden bridges which were used up to the mid-18th century, were unstable and prone to failure. The first issue was the expense replacement of them every 20 years if the wood began to decay or was unstable was excessive. The most often, it required the stopping of trains for a period. Brick bridges are stronger and lasted longer, they were expensive. Through his new patent, Carnegie could make wrought iron, and then make it sturdy enough to support trains forever. Keystone Bridge Company Keystone Bridge Company was the instrument using which Carnegie would use the newly developed technology.

The very first venture that Keystone set out on was the building of his Eads Bridge spanning across the Mississippi River in 1867. It would be the biggest bridge ever built in America and also the most costly project he'd undertaken so to this point. However, it was his mentor and ally Thomas Scott who had helped to win the contract as well as the cash he hoped to gain from it led him to look at new methods of raising capital. Over the period of five years, between 1867-1872 He travelled across Europe selling bonds for the bridge as well as the tracks for railways that will be crossing it. He was able to raise enough funds to finance the construction and he even made a amount in commissions.

In the following decade around, Carnegie won contracts to create bridges throughout the nation. Certain bridges are smaller than Eads Bridge, were built during the time between construction of the Eads and were unveiled prior to the bridge was completed.

This comprised those of the Hannibal Bridge over the Missouri River in Kansas City, Keokuk Rail Bridge that crosses Keokuk Rail Bridge that crosses the Mississippi River at Keokuk, Iowa and Keokuk Rail Bridge crossing the Mississippi River in Iowa, and Windsor Harbor Road Bridge at Kimmswick in Missouri.

To boost public perception of bridges which had gained the reputation of being prone to the possibility of collapse, Carnegie used a publicity campaign that involved an elephant being allowed to travel across bridges constructed in Keystone Bridge Company. Keystone Bridge Company. Between bridges and railroads built by him within his huge holdings from the middle of the 1860s, Carnegie made a very large impact on the transport business throughout America. For his transport business the way Carnegie conducted business was very traditional. Carnegie was member of several firms that helped him make his mark on railroads and bridges, whereas Vanderbilt as well as J.P. Morgan (discussed below) who pounced on pre-made companies and were given the snide name "robber barons". Apart from a lack of understanding of the significance of high-quality iron during the construction of the Eads Bridge The reputation of Carnegie's adherence to high-quality work did not go unnoticed.

J. P. Morgan

John Piermont Morgan was the most successful banker. In his long professional career, he excelled of entering and acquiring the most successful companies to enhance their performance. Sometimes Morgan would help troubled companies and transform them with a stringent method of cutting backs, layoffs and then repurposing the business to become "Morganization". The strength of Morgan, being a former banker was his ability to mobilize investments funds. He spent the initial 12 years of his life working for his father's bank company. Through this time the young man learned all that he required to know about investing banking. The year was 1869 when Morgan decided to concentrate at investing in companies. The field he chose was not surprising, as it was one of the largest industries in America during the entire second period in the nineteenth century: railroads.

The entry is sounded with an explosion

The Albany and Susquehanna Railroad was nowhere on the list of the most remarkable railroads in America during the 1860s. It ran just 35 miles long, and it connected two cities that were small within the State of New York; Albany and Brighton. It also linked with four other railroads, which stretched across to the New England states to the coal mines in Pennsylvania. It had a lot possibilities as a linking railroad and set up a power struggle between two camps. One composed of financial gurus Jay Gould and Jim Fisk while the other consists of railroad chief Joseph H. Ramsey and his top executives.

The fight, was played out on the New York State corridors of the law and power as well as in the national press, covered by both national and state newspapers. The year was 1869. Morgan was able to intervene at the requests by Joseph Ramsey, who conspired to give him the status of the majority shareholder in order to prevent Fisk and Gould from taking control of the railway. Morgan put in over fifty thousand dollars (about 14 million today in dollars) to hold the largest stake, and to force an election. Morgan was elected vice-president for the railroad. He was successful in taking authority over the railway by Gould and Fisk The following year Morgan sold all its assets for the Delaware and Hudson Canal Company.

Through the entire 1870s, Morgan acted as the most reliable investor of the railway industry throughout America. Working together with Peabody at the start of his bank career and was able access capital from rich in cash British banks and create the fastest expansion of American railways. However, these ventures came with a cost that required him take part with the running of the railroad after it was constructed. The railroads which were not efficient were revamped and modernized to increase efficient operation. He was adamant about a better integrated transportation system across America and used funds to ensure that his vision came true.

Walking paths with Vanderbilt

In 1883, Cornelius Vanderbilt had been dead for six years. He had left the son William to oversee his huge railroad empire. In order to connect the various railroads that were operating throughout New York City, Vanderbilt ordered the construction of a central station in central New York. It also set out in a massive expansion plan, gaining access to The Great Lakes Region to the North West as far as Illinois up to the west.

Much capital was required for the expansion and until 1883, the difficulty in raising capital was holding William behind. J.P. Morgan did not struggle to raise money however he was not a professional with knowledge of running railroads. His specialization was in financing. A sort of partnership was established in which Morgan took in the funds and William took over the construction and operating of new railroad lines. William was instrumental in helping William acquire his responsibility for the West Shore Railroad that had competed against its New York Central company since the time he was able to take charge of the operation from his father.

With William, Morgan had found an employee who he was comfortable working with. He was ambitious, hardworking and eager to work hard required to be dominant. The key was not just to have a desire to win and be able to work hard for it and to achieve it, that made a difference to Morgan. It was the idea of competition that seemed to be undervalued for a man who worked his entire life to achieve the best performance possible, and his team members towards similar goals as well.

In order to convince William to buy West Shore Railroad, West Shore Railroad, Morgan was forced to employ an extremely unconventional and well-known method. Morgan invited William as well as the executives of West Shore aboard his yacht and set sail on Hudson. He was unable to return to port if there was no agreement and compelled the two sides to come to a compromise.

Another railroad Morgan and Vanderbilt were working on together included that of the Chesapeake and Ohio Railway. It was a major cargo railroad which served the coal fields in West Virginia, the C&O proved to be very successful being an affiliated company to Vanderbilt's New York Central Railway. Being a shareholder controlling the company, Morgan could stop the railroad from expanding to his territory. In the eyes of Morgan it was the perfect investment opportunity to pass up.

The railroad industry is poised to consolidate industry

After investing millions of dollars in the railway business, Morgan realized that the available capital was making the railroads inefficient. Therefore, he was the advocate of consolidation and reorganization. When railways that were well-run operated along with ineffective railways, Morgan would facilitate the purchase of weak railroads by the stronger. He did this through negotiating with to get the New York Central to acquire the West Shore railroads in 1885.

But he wasn't willing to let well-run railroads go down in order to keep his grip on important routes as well as markets. As an example, after assisting with the Philadelphia and Reading Railway reorganize in 1886. He then halted the work of its director in order to transform it into the status of a national railroad just two years after. For Morgan his cash, it permitted him to determine which business could be permitted to grow and which could be destined for be an ailing regional railway. Sadly for Reading Line The dice came up with the second.

Morgan's involvement in railroads during the early 1890s was cut by the US Congress approved the Interstate Commerce Act in 1887. From 1890 onwards, Morgan organized industry conferences which brought together senior executives of all major railroads in the United States. The goal was to establish an enlightened framework to ensure the protection of the interests of all stakeholders by ensuring that there were reasonable and stable rates within the railway industry. The efforts of his were likely to save railway transport from battling itself out of competition.

Northern Pacific Railway

The North Pacific Railway was a highly strategic railroad because it linked the Atlantic Pacific and Atlantic Oceans on the same track. The only railroad that could be able to boast this achievement. It was commissioned by the US government in 1864, and began operations in 1870, the railroad changed hands multiple times during its construction until its inception on 1883. The railroad was first very close to bankruptcy during 1873. It was but it was able to escape, only to fall into financial trouble again before declaring bankruptcy in 1875. In 1893 it declared bankruptcy twice. time.

The railroad's federal ownership as well as interstate connectivity will be an problem. Three different supreme courts within where the railroad had its operations struggled to stop the bankruptcies. The employees were not paid because a administrator was not appointed. This was such a ferocious conflict it was that US Army had to be in place to defend its property.

Morgan used all his influencers in an effort to have the job of managing this portion of the North Pacific turned over to his. Morgan had already earned an image of successfully helping struggling railroads recover after the panic of 1893 making it simpler to convince railway's shareholders to allow him to take over as receiver of the business. The receiver was basically given the power to acquire Northern Pacific for himself and as the government was deciding to erase all obligations Northern Pacific owed, Morgan effectively took over a debt-free business.

www.ingramcontent.com/pod-product-compliance
Lightning Source LLC
Chambersburg PA
CBHW070555010526
44118CB00012B/1332